SydelineWorks Sweeties
Amora Diamond

Ordering Information:

Tia Tormen Productions
P.O. Box 8069
Pittsburgh, PA 15216

Contact tiatormen@yahoo.com

Printed in the
United States of America

ISB-13# 978-0-9859354-1-2

ISBN-10# 0985935413

First Edition

Presenting.................

Amora Diamond

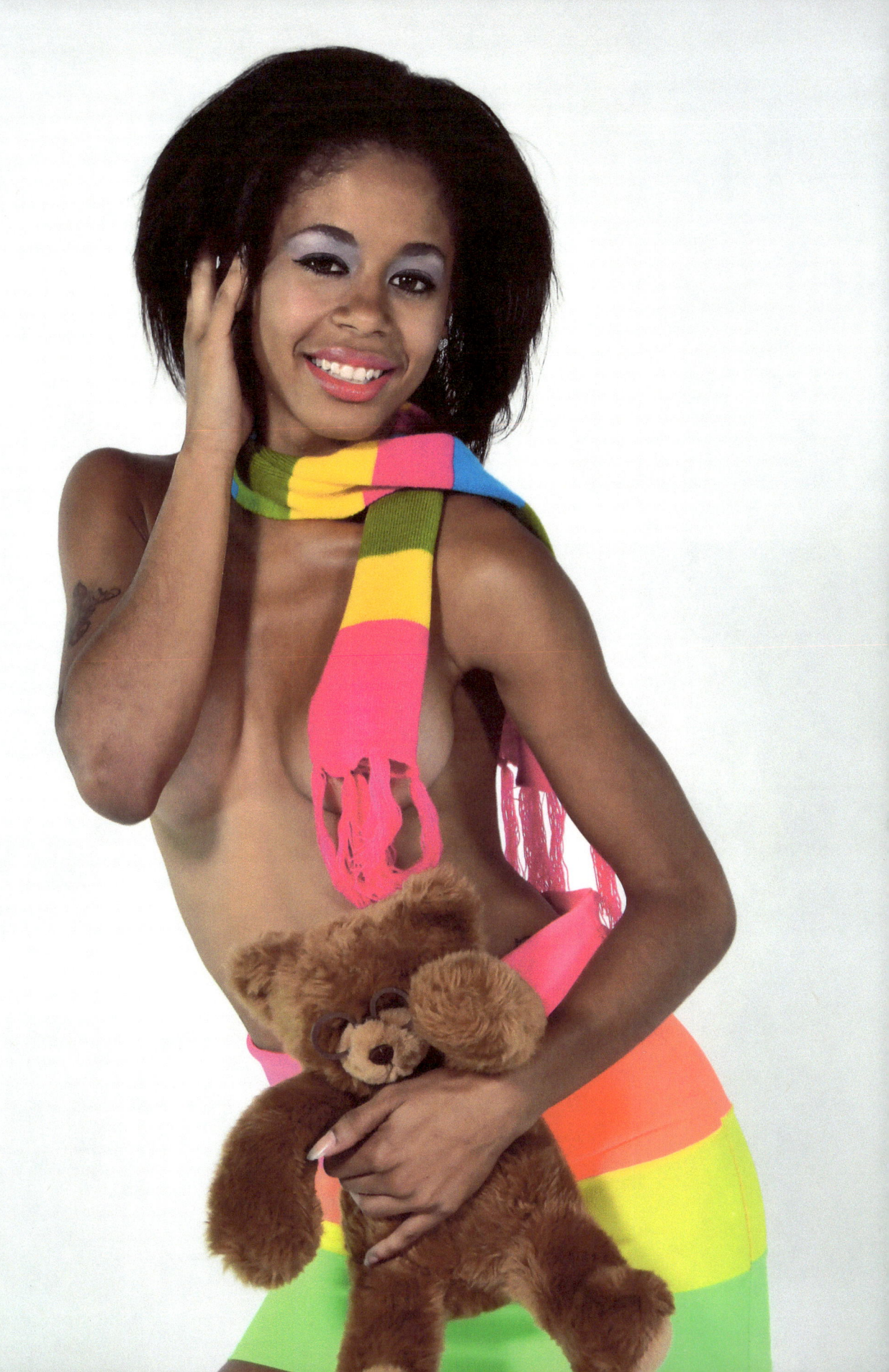

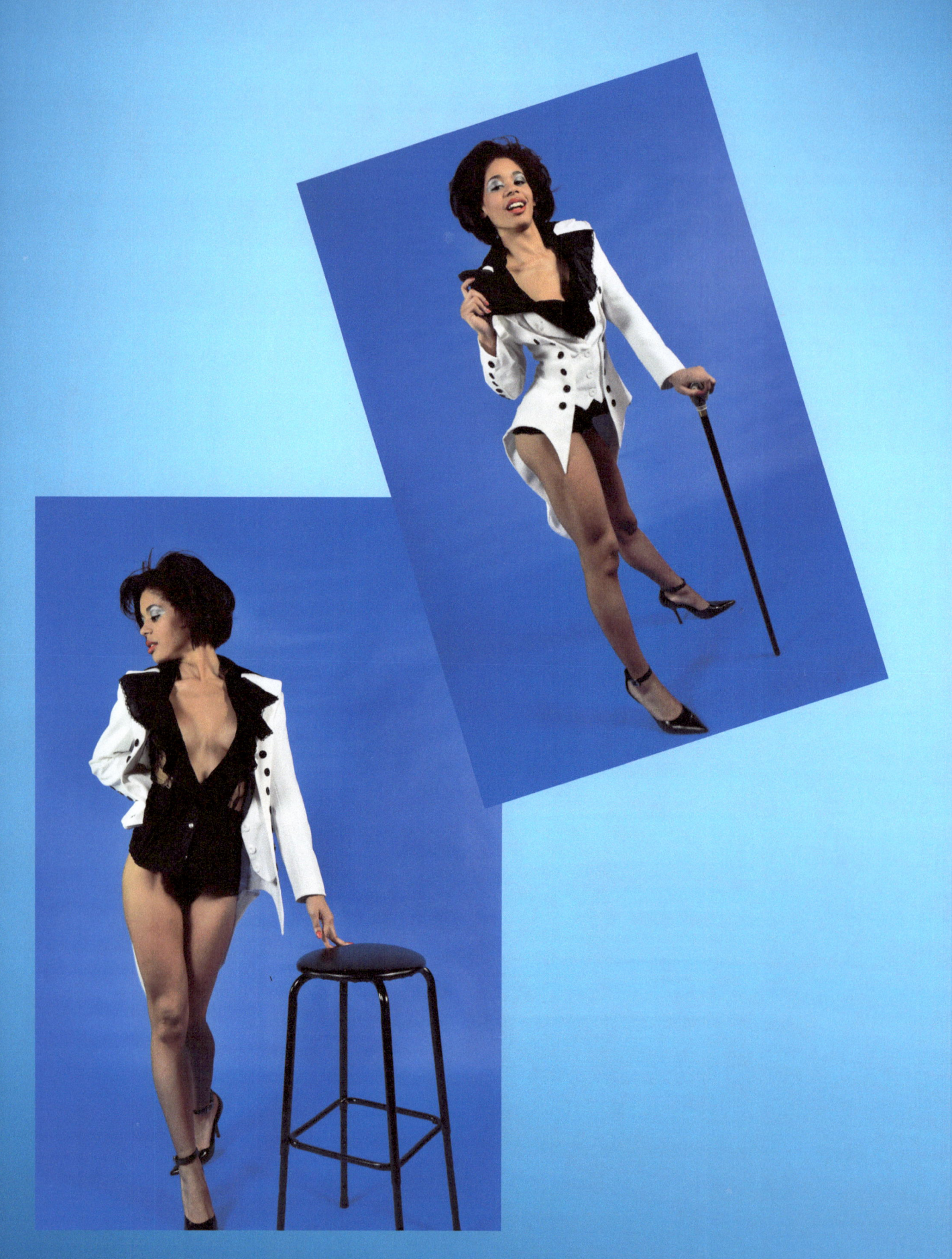

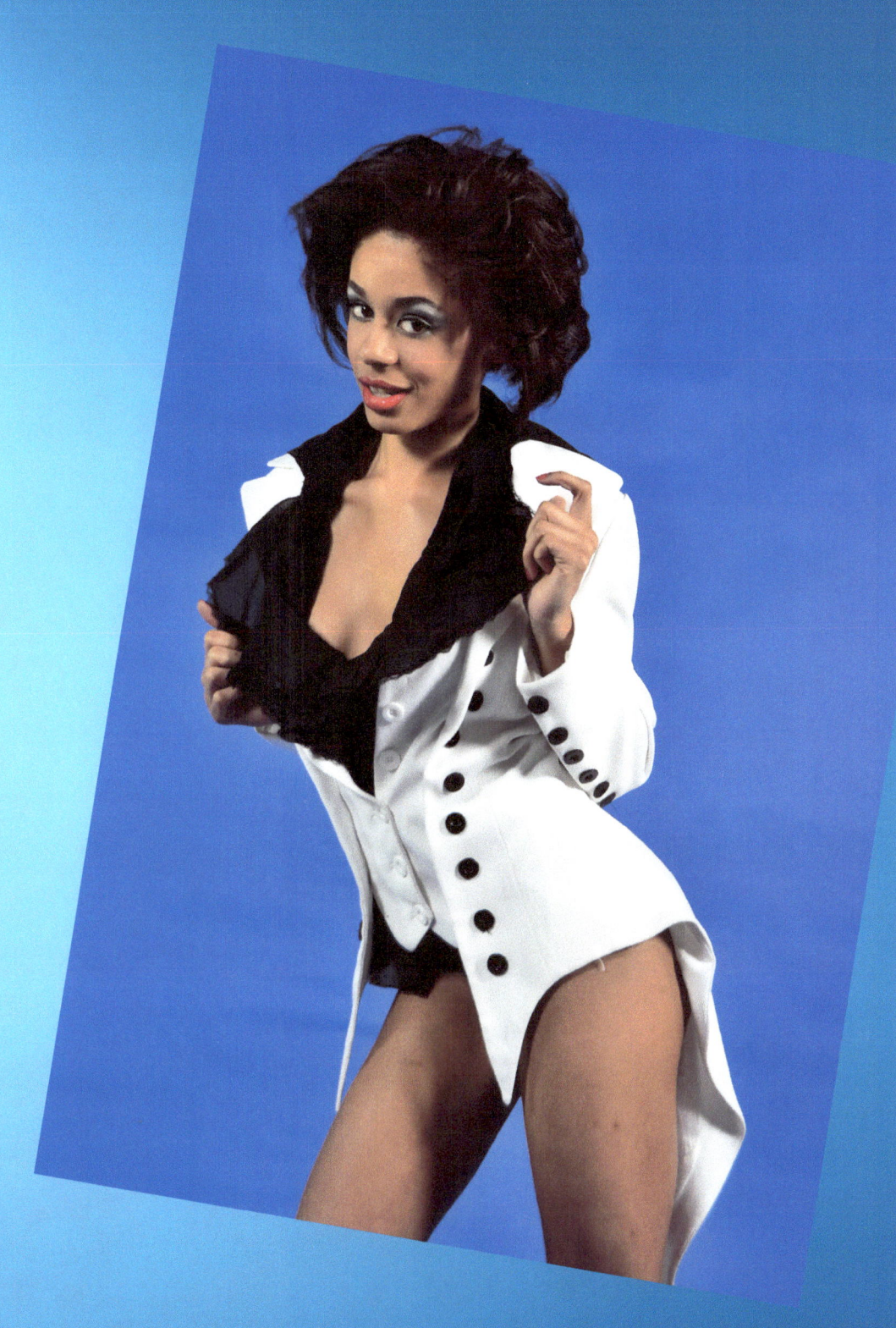

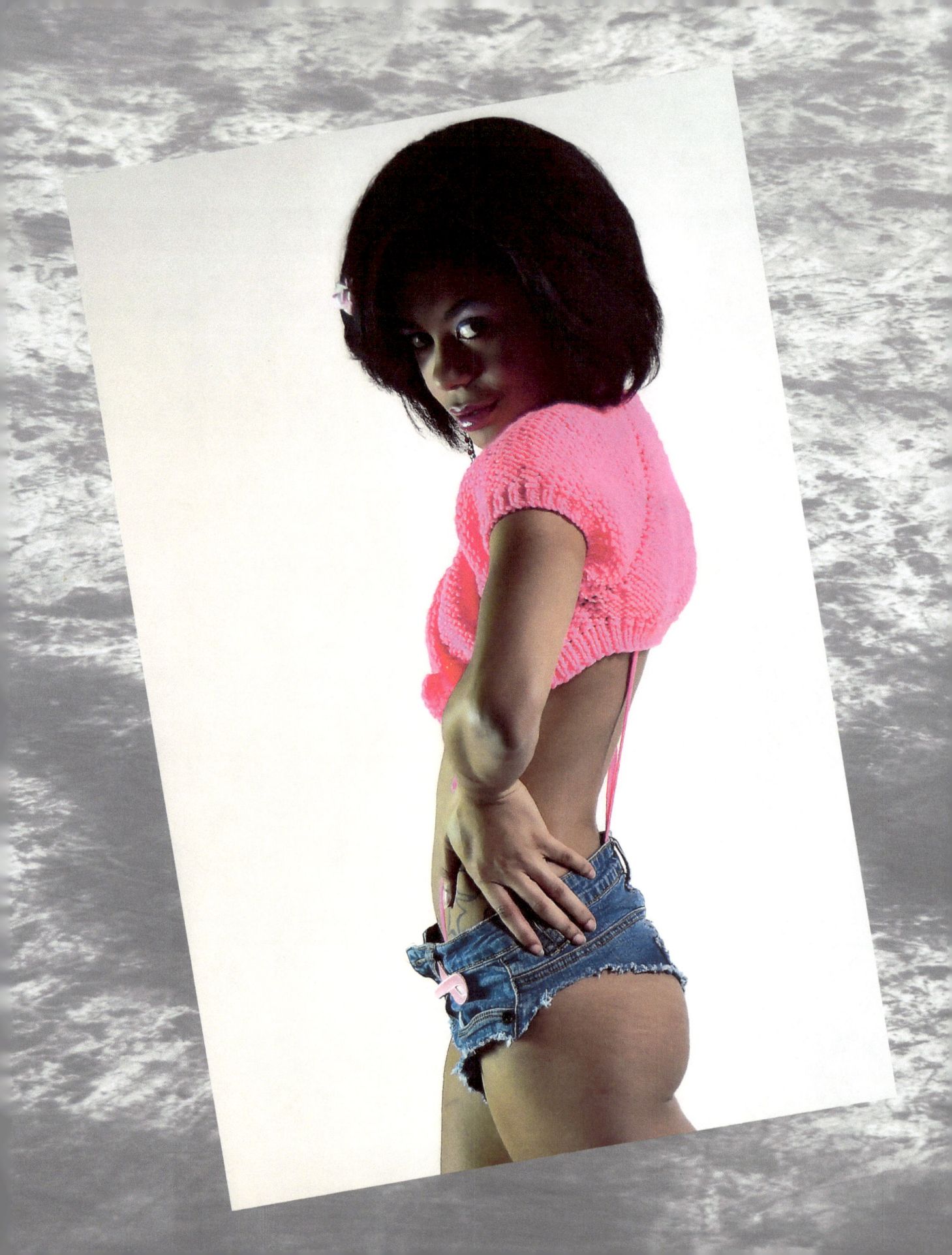

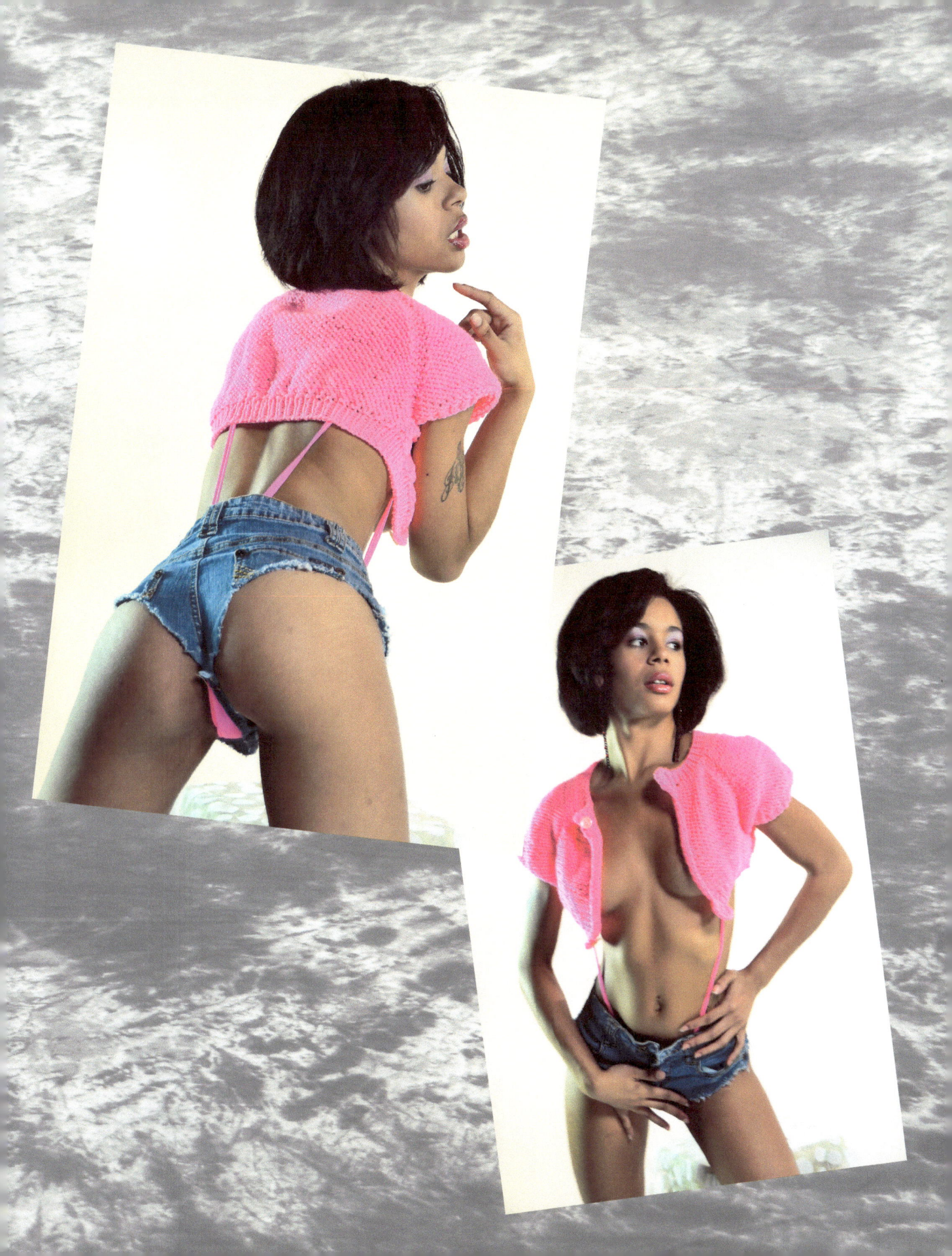

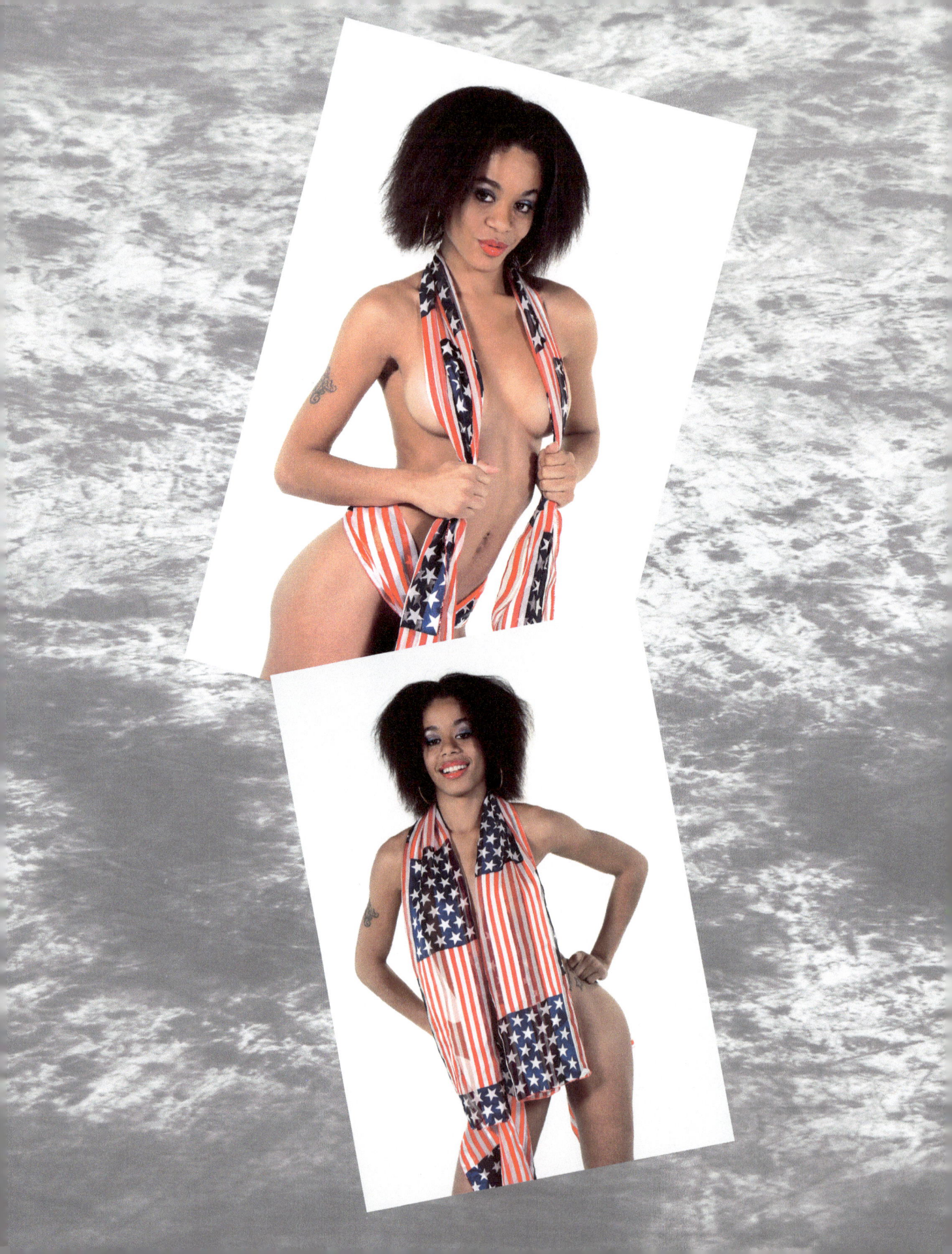

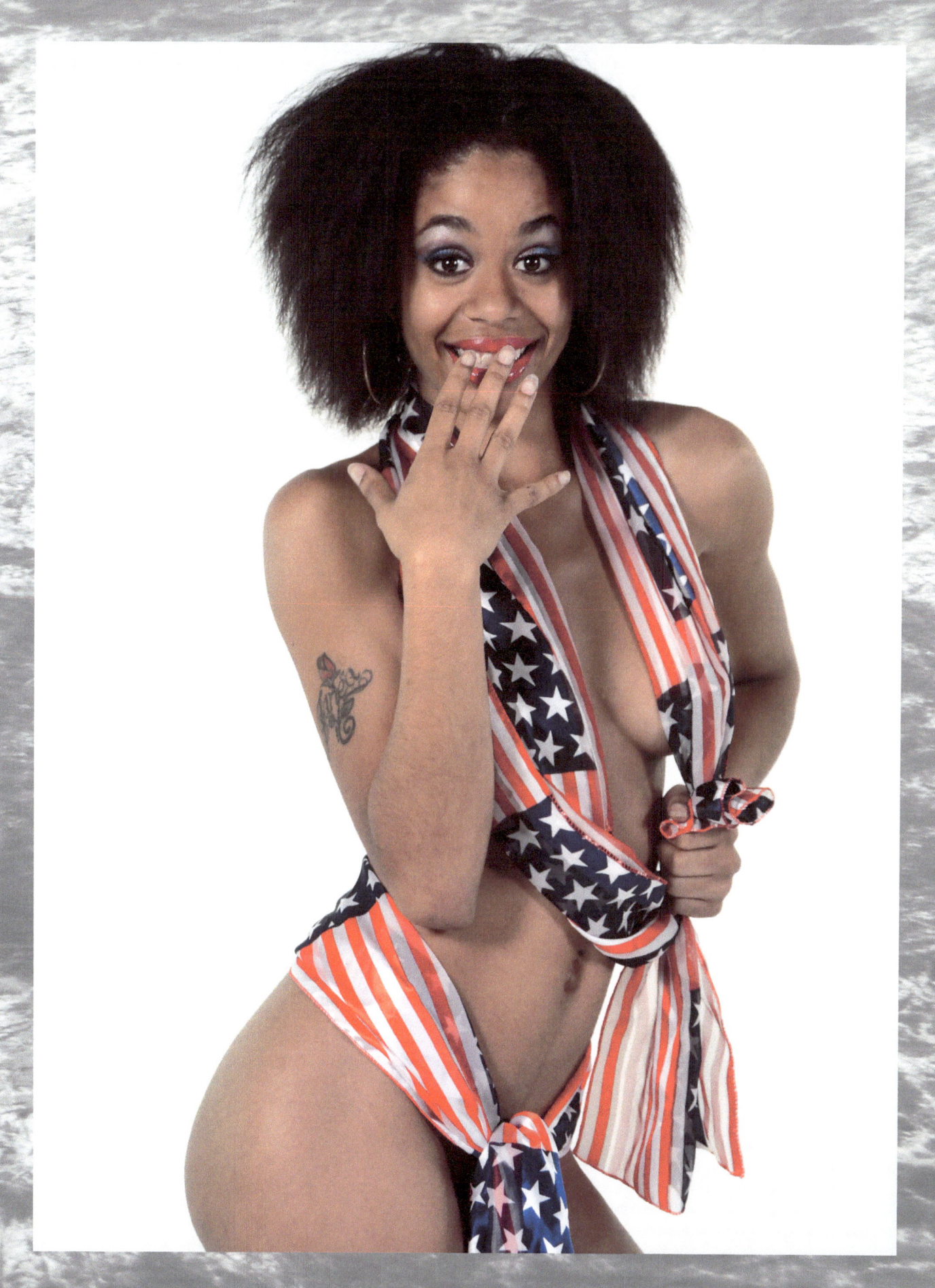

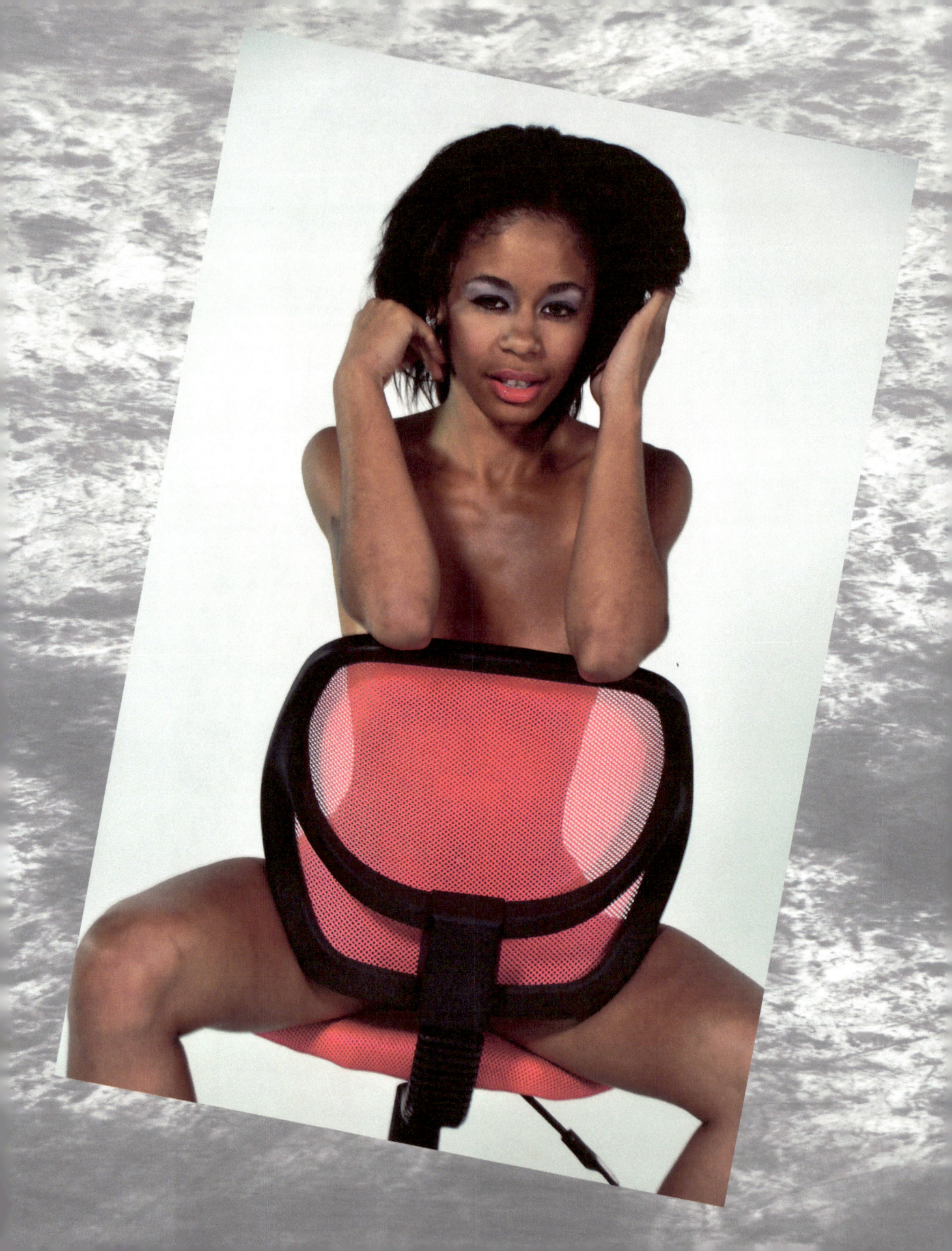

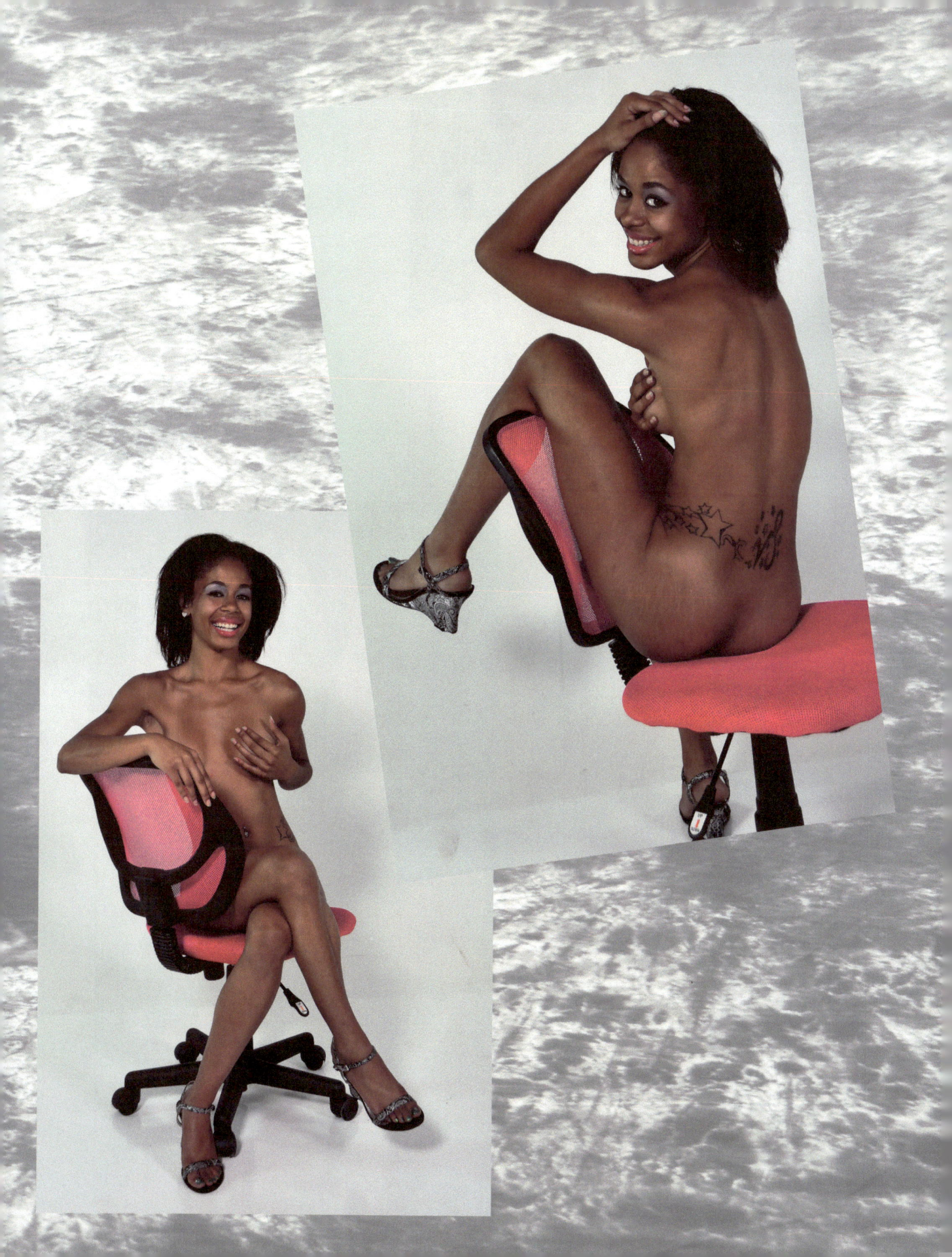

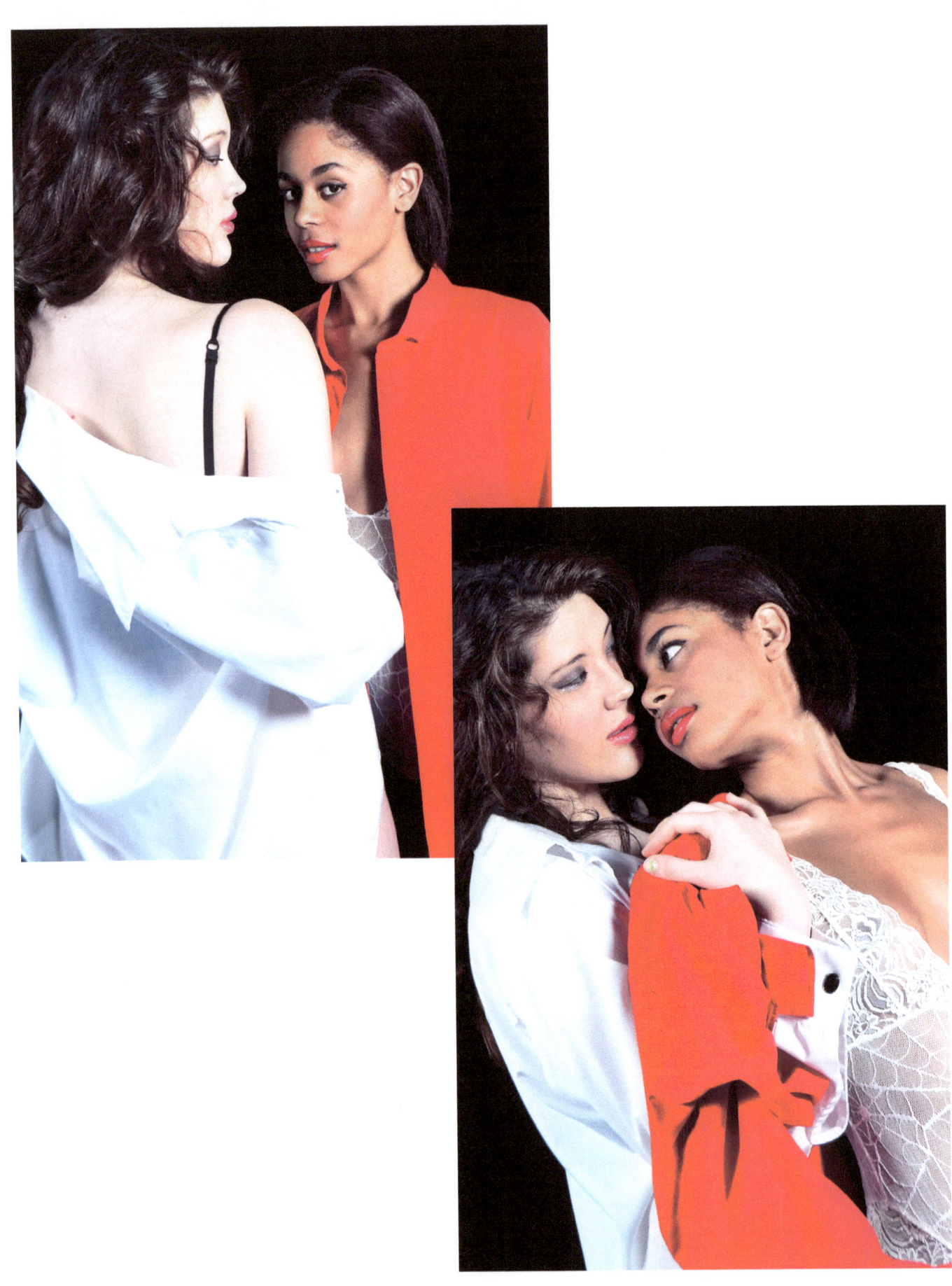

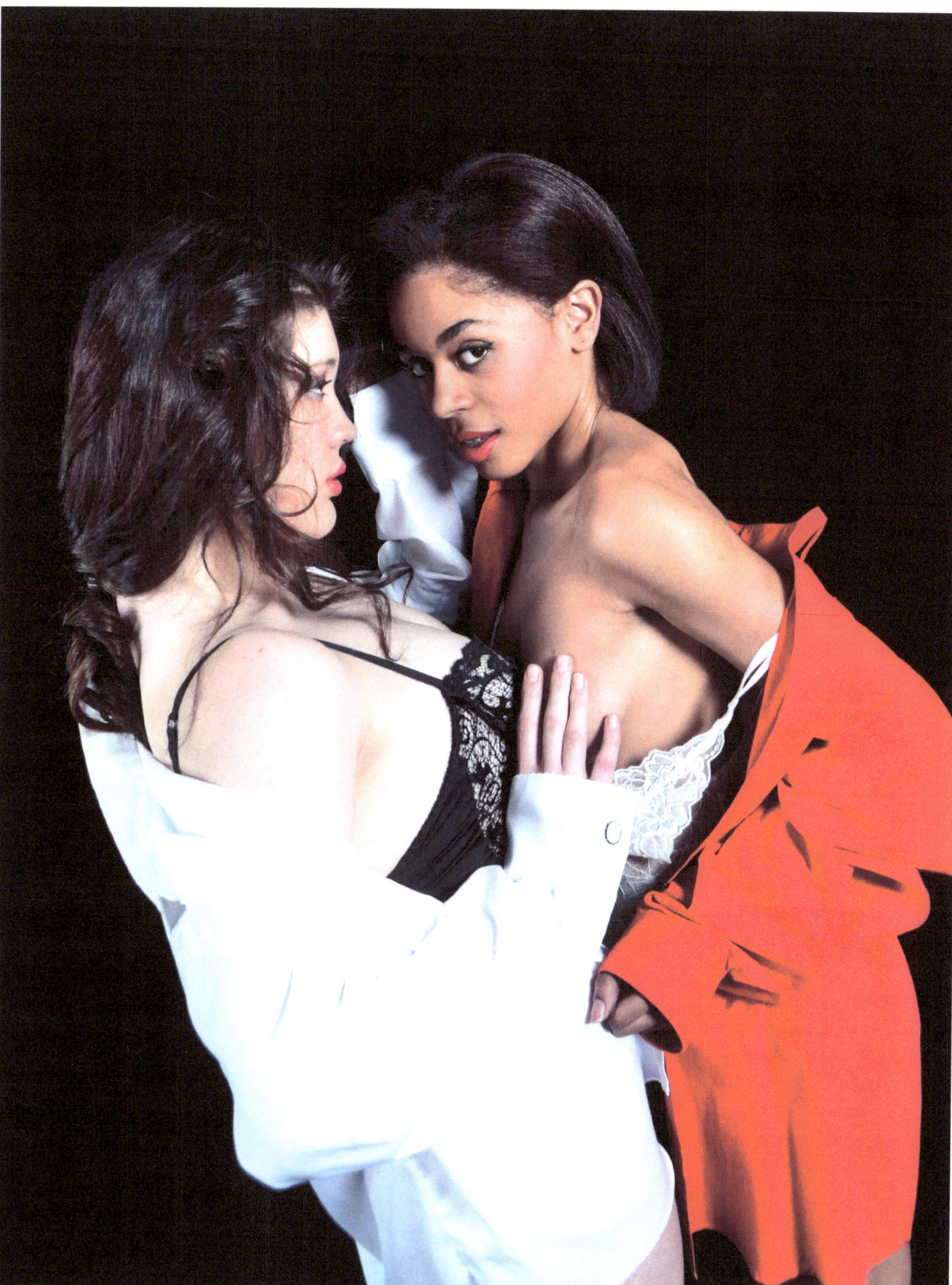

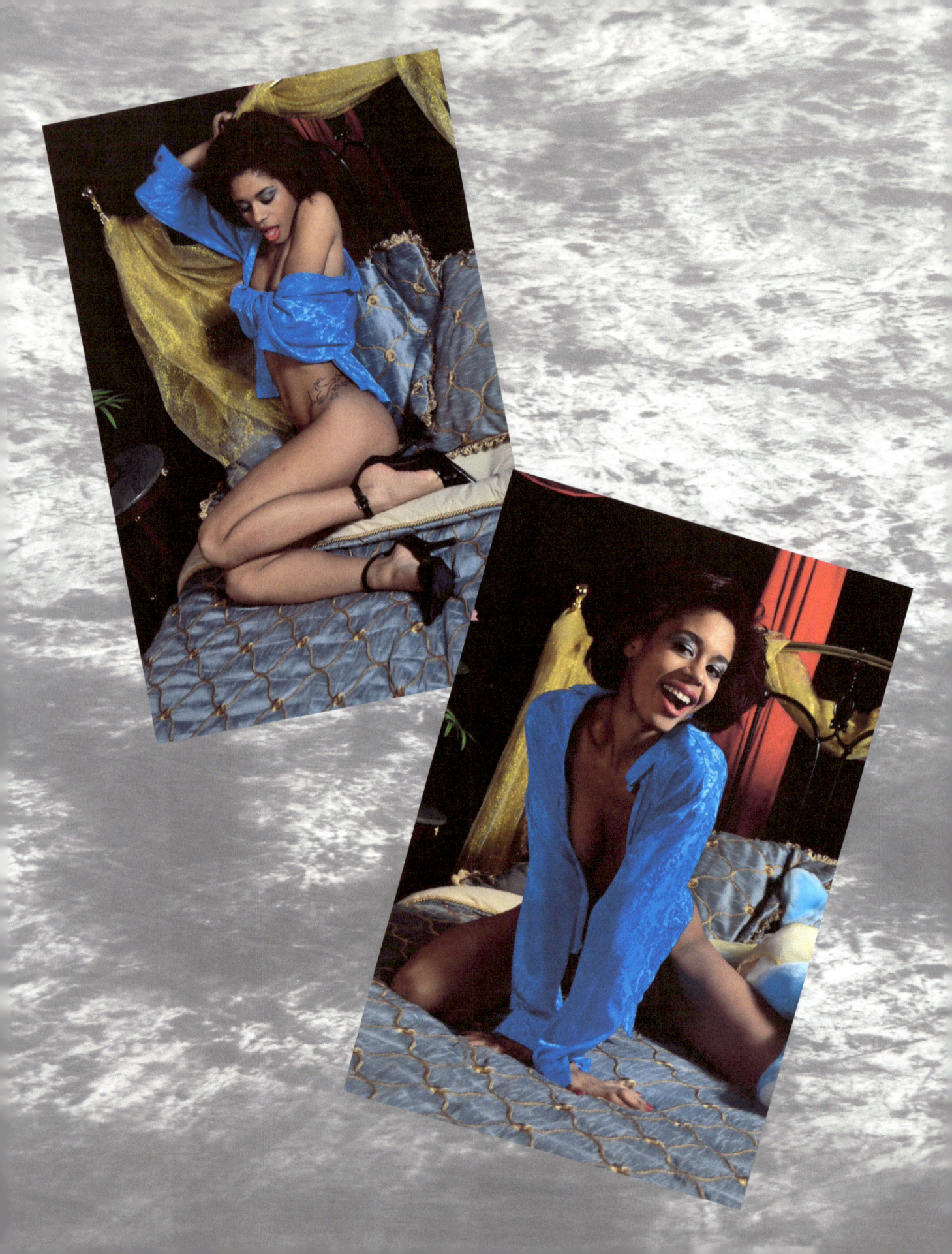

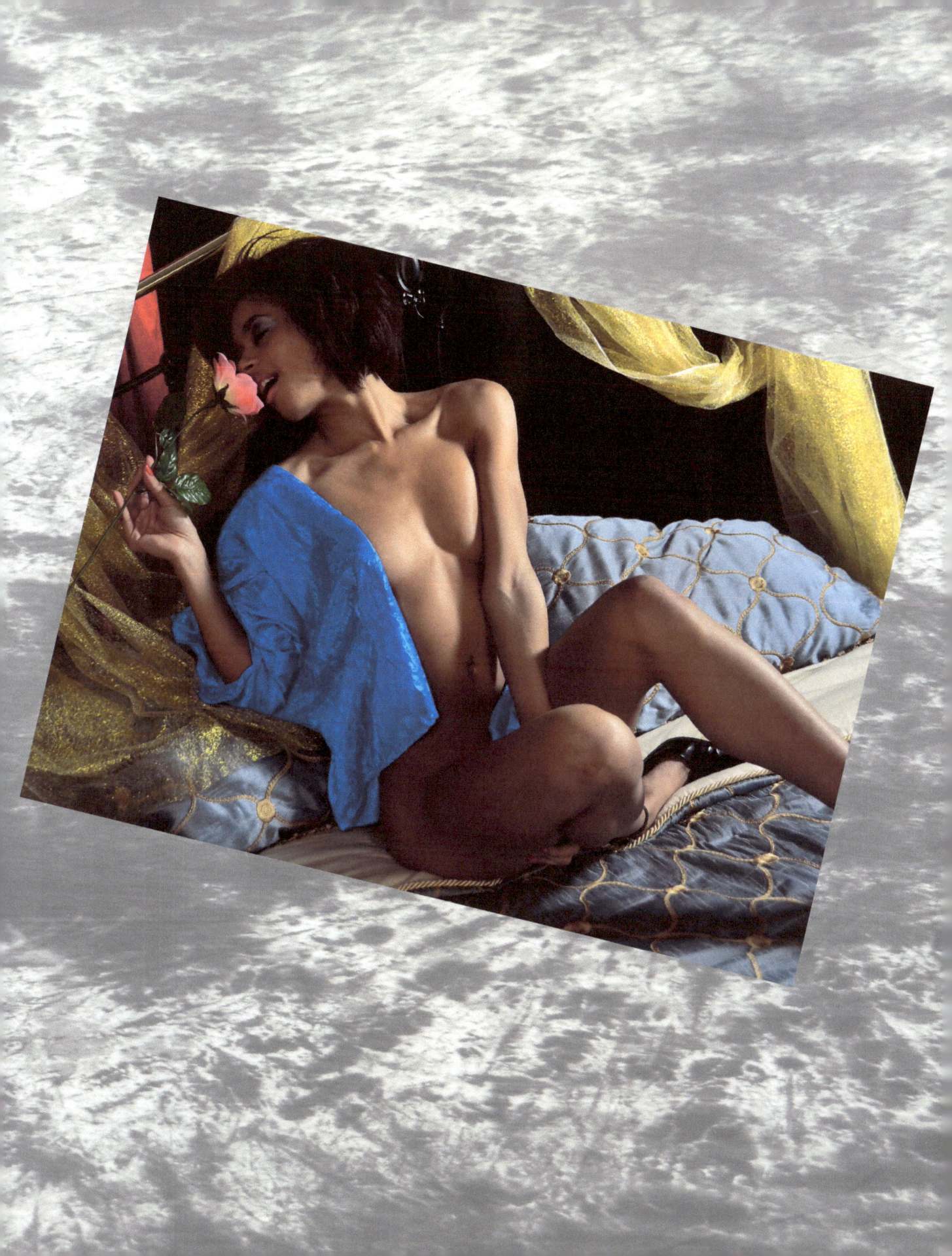

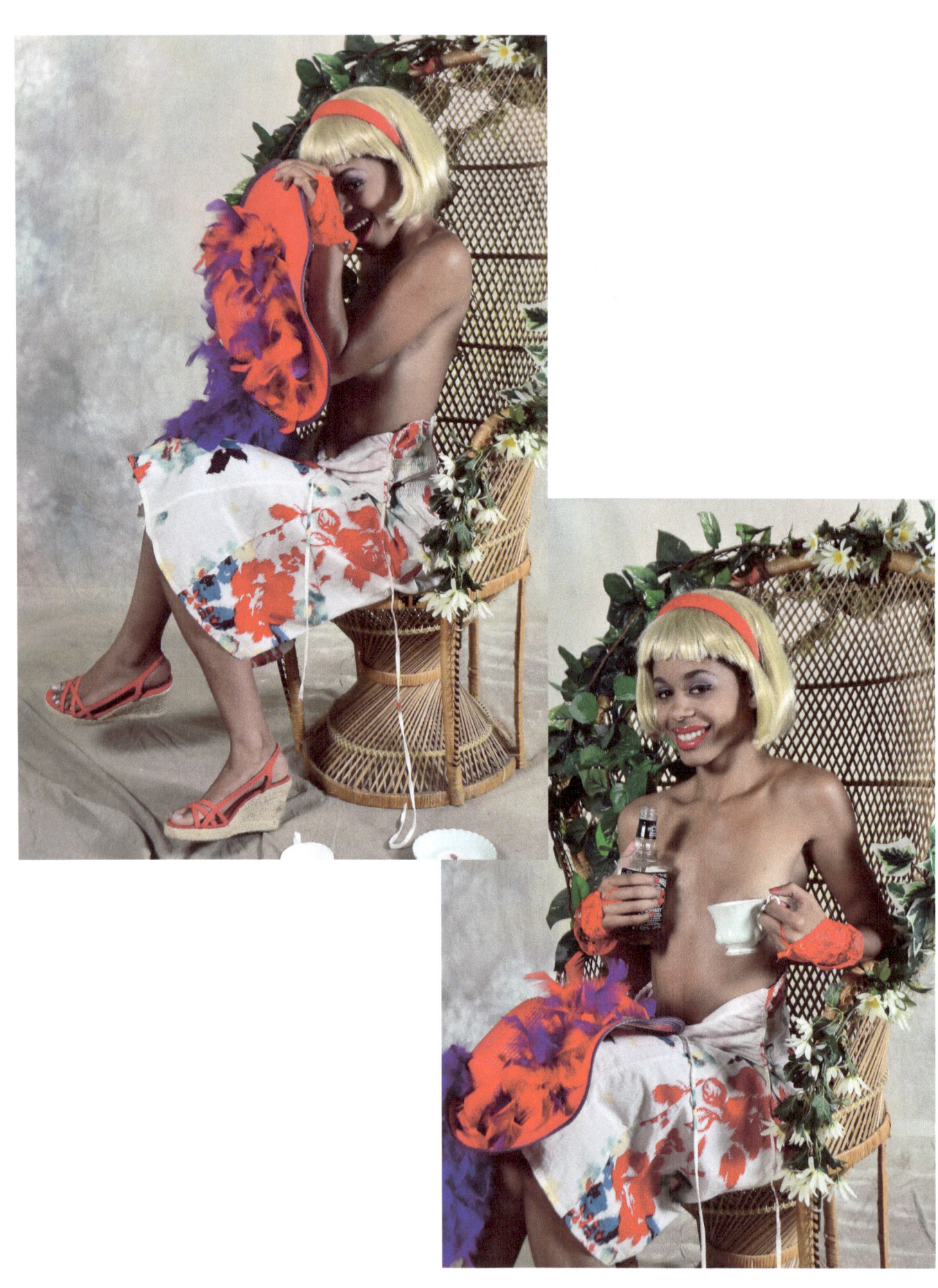

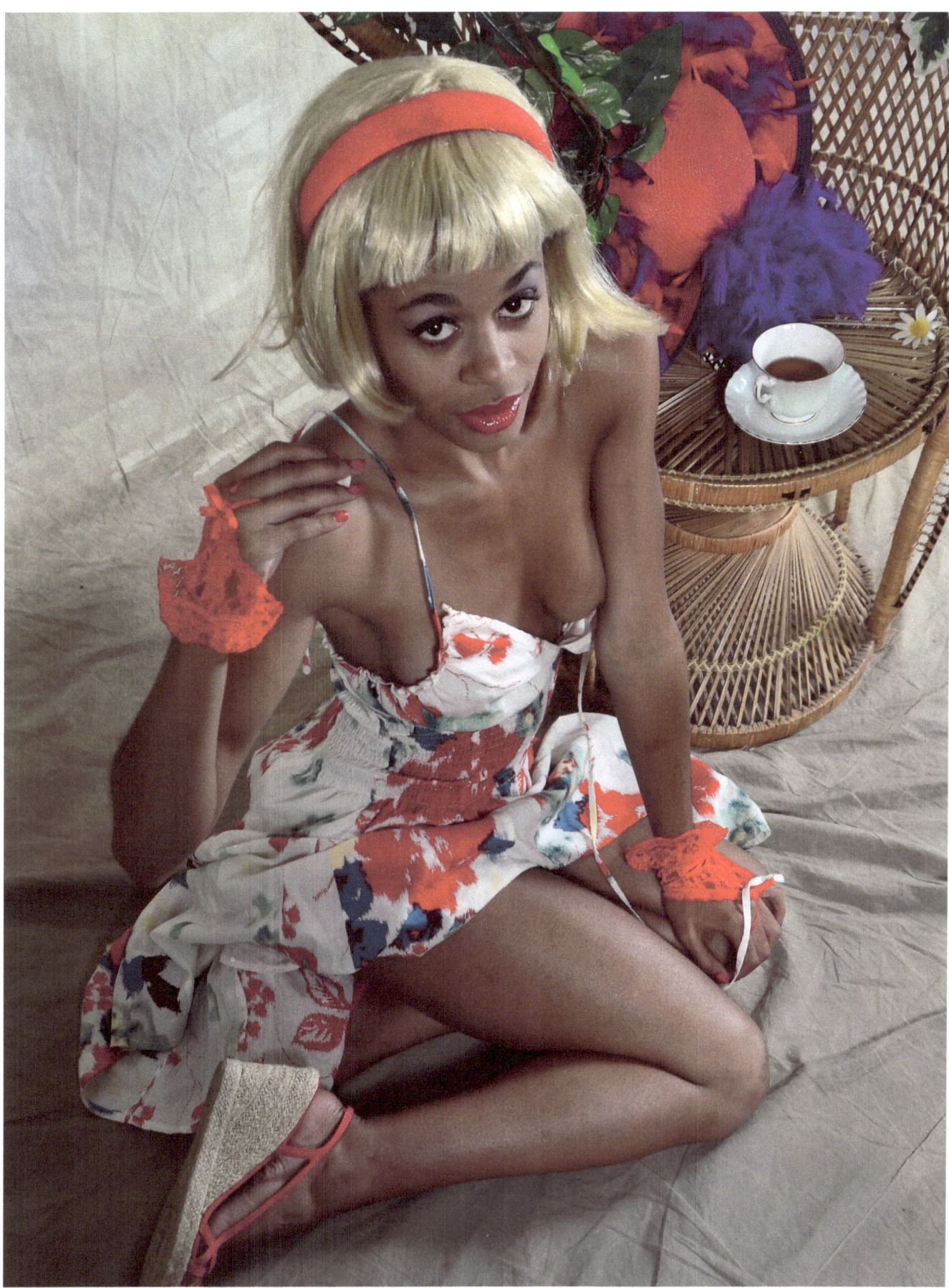

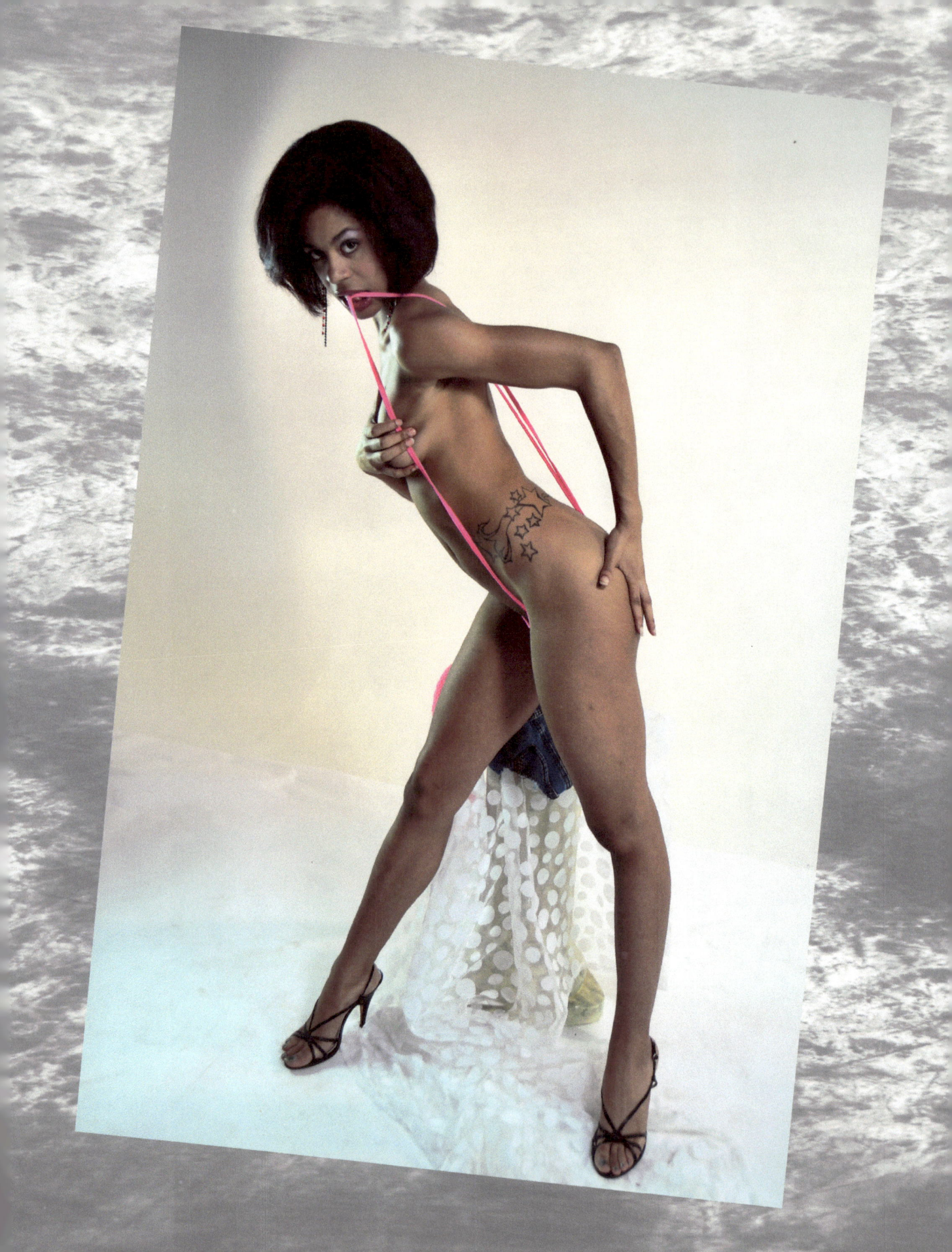

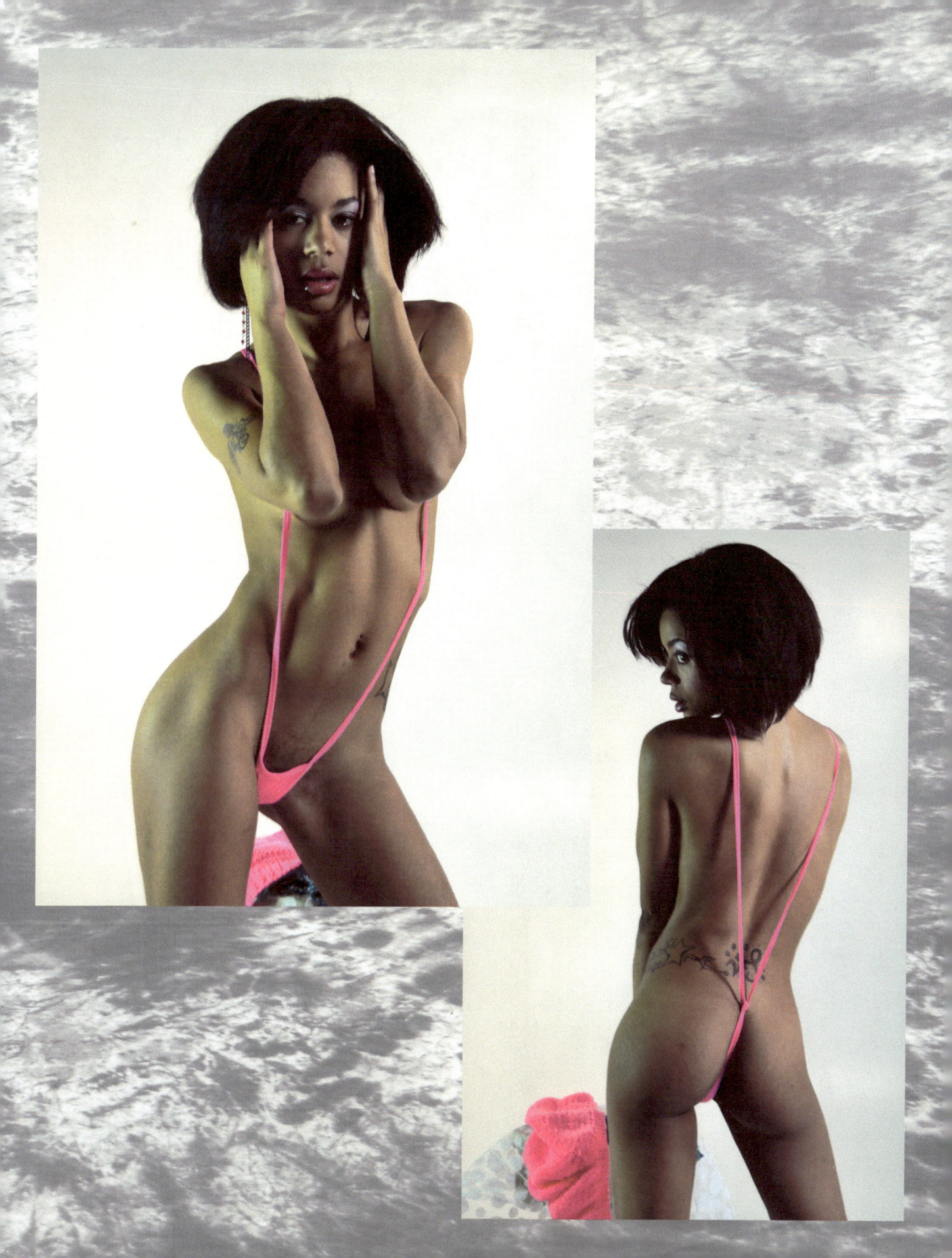

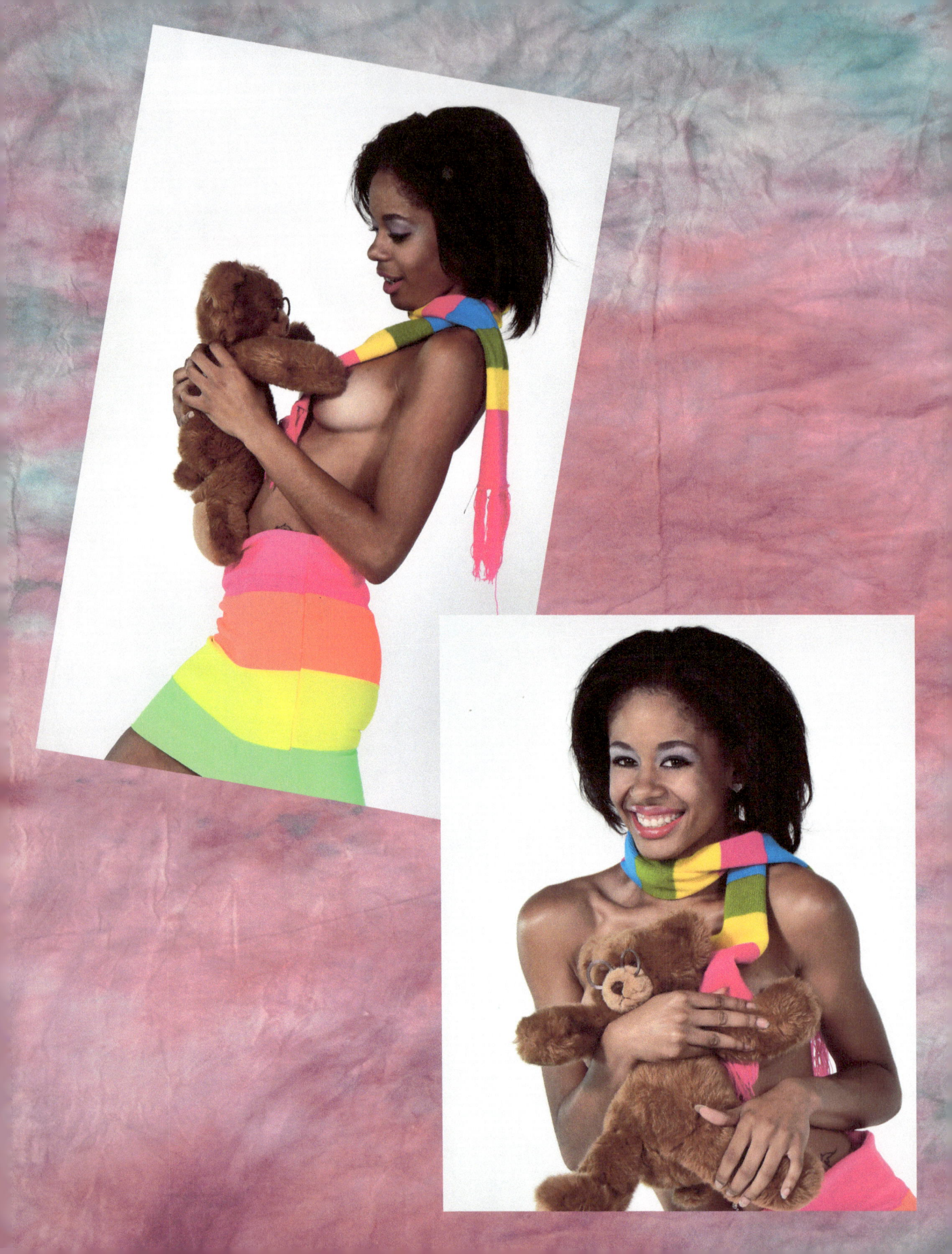

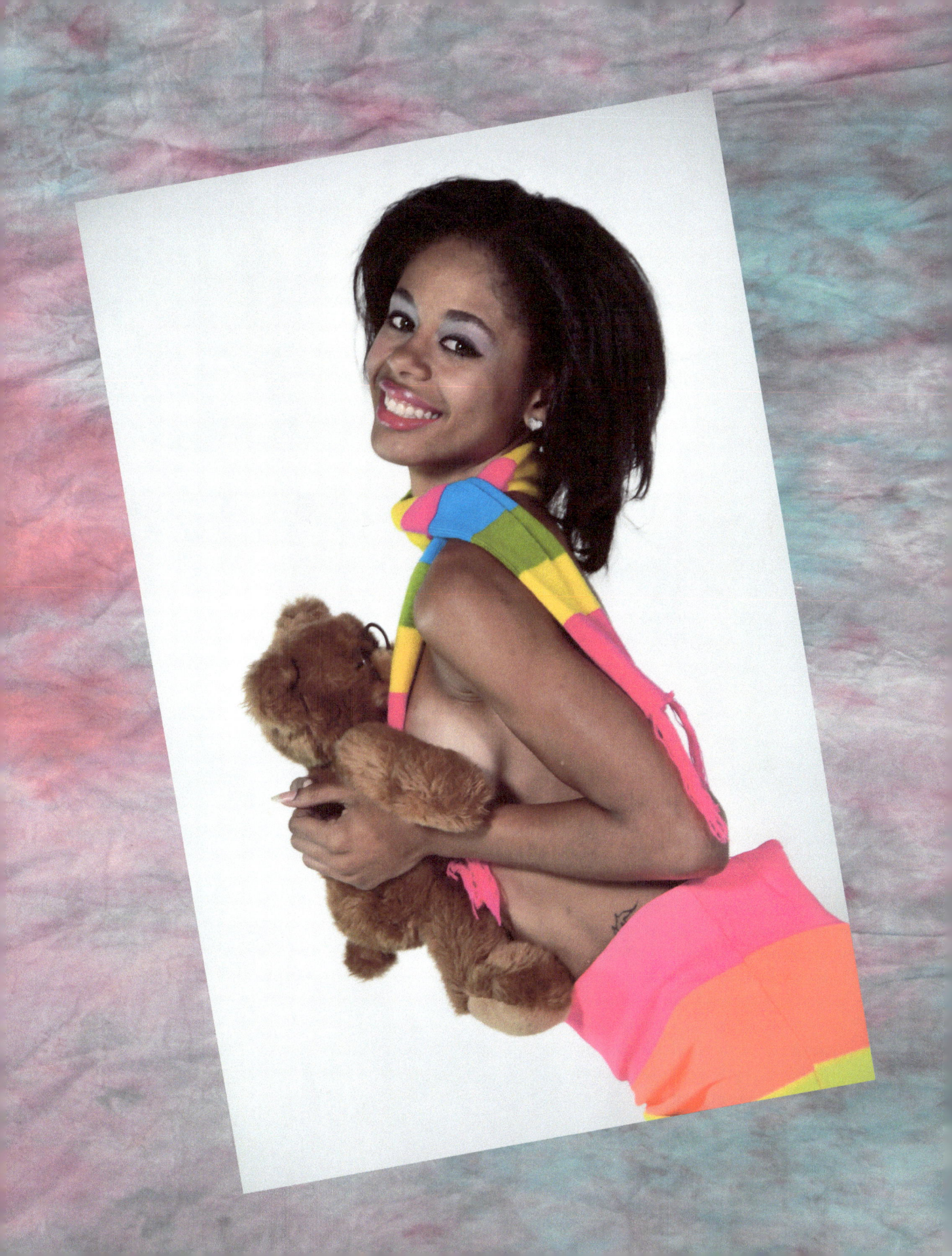

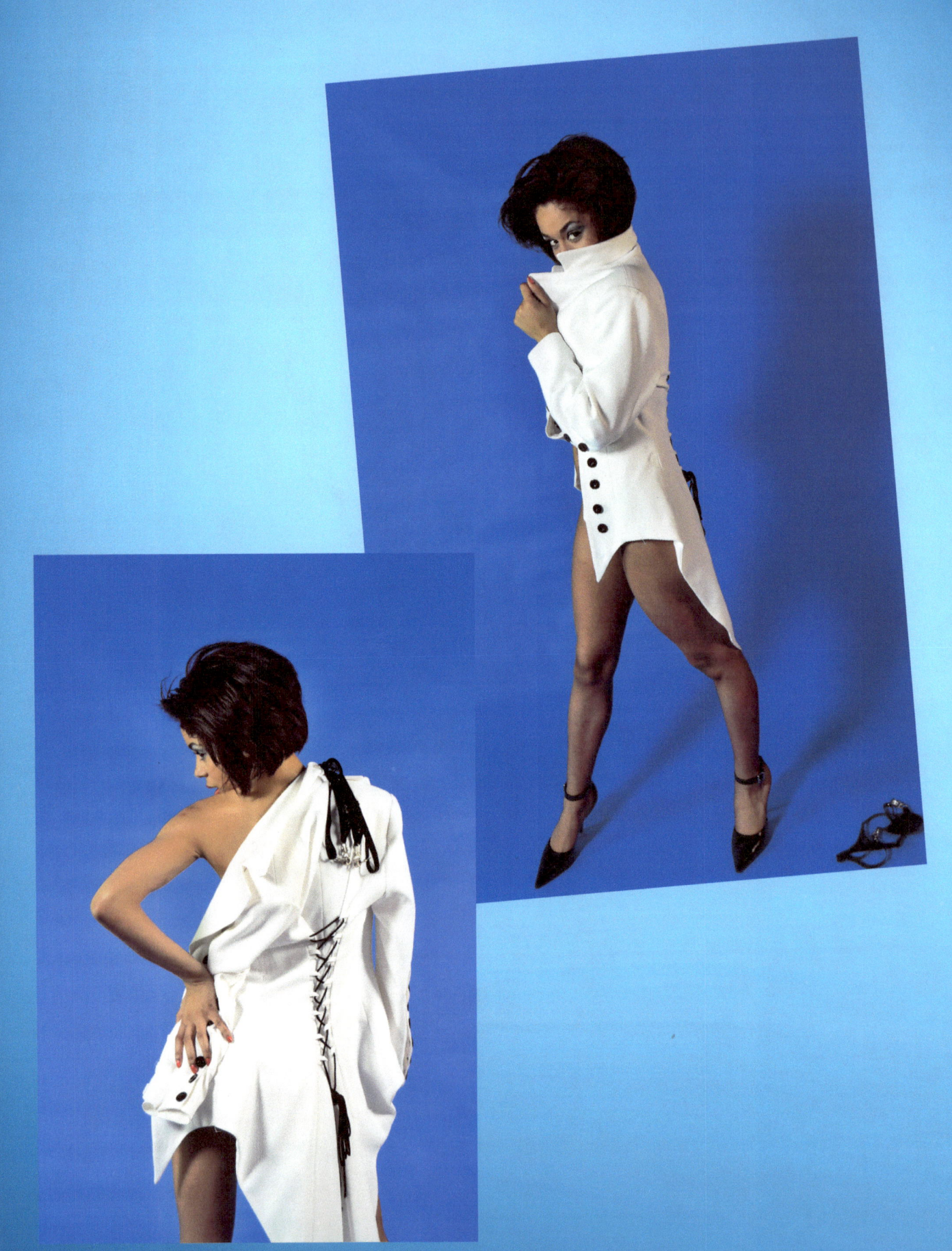

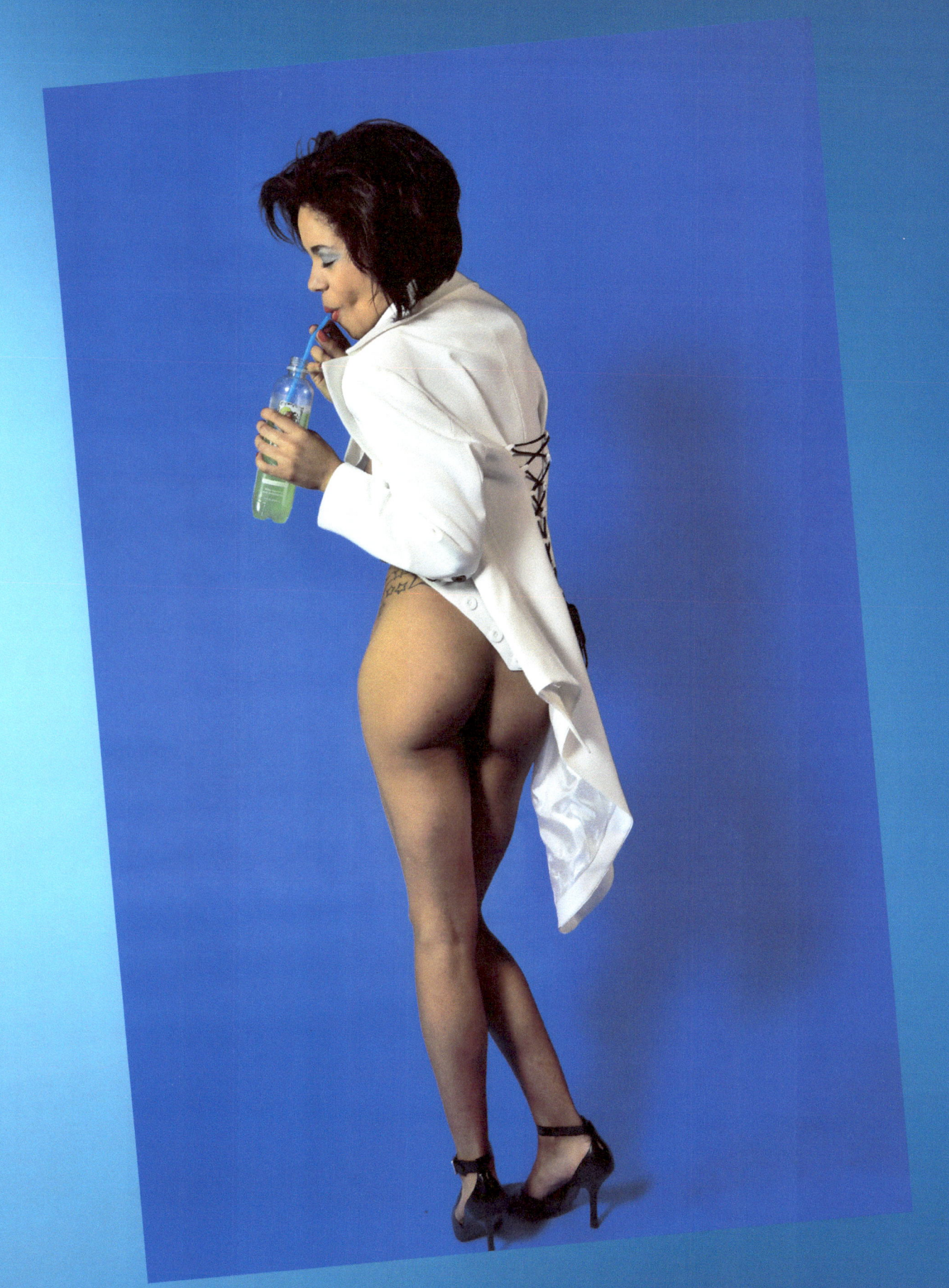

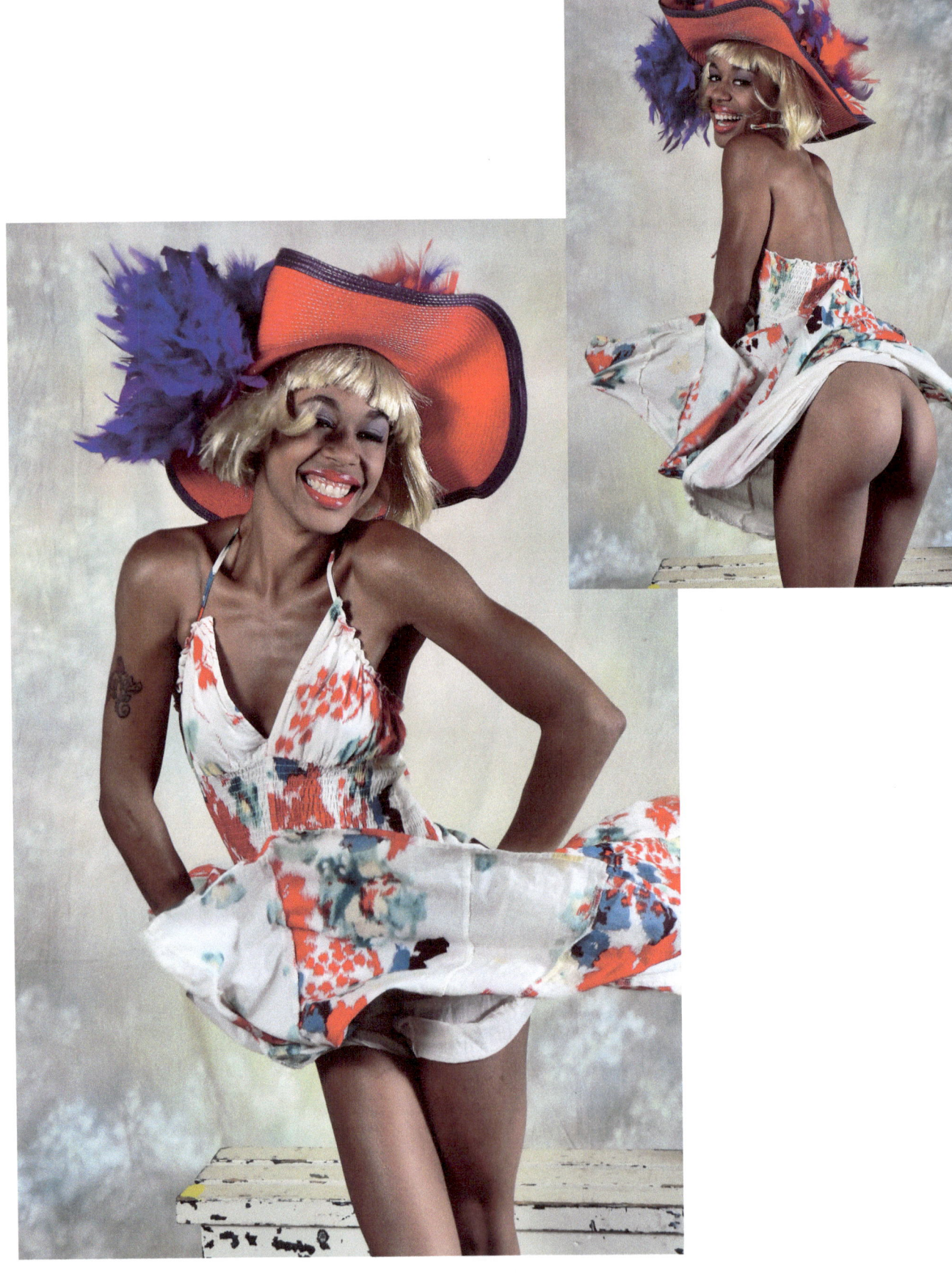

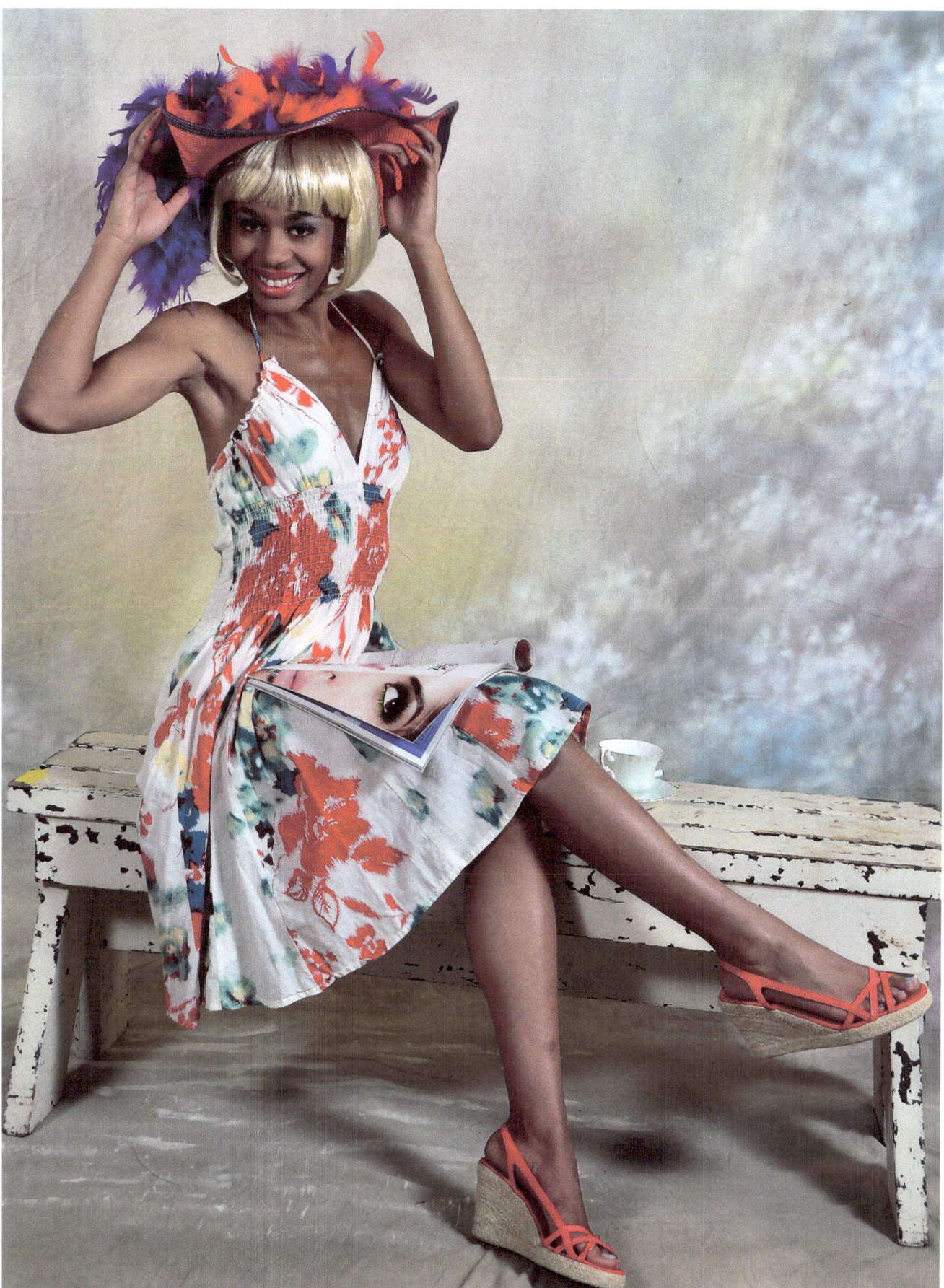

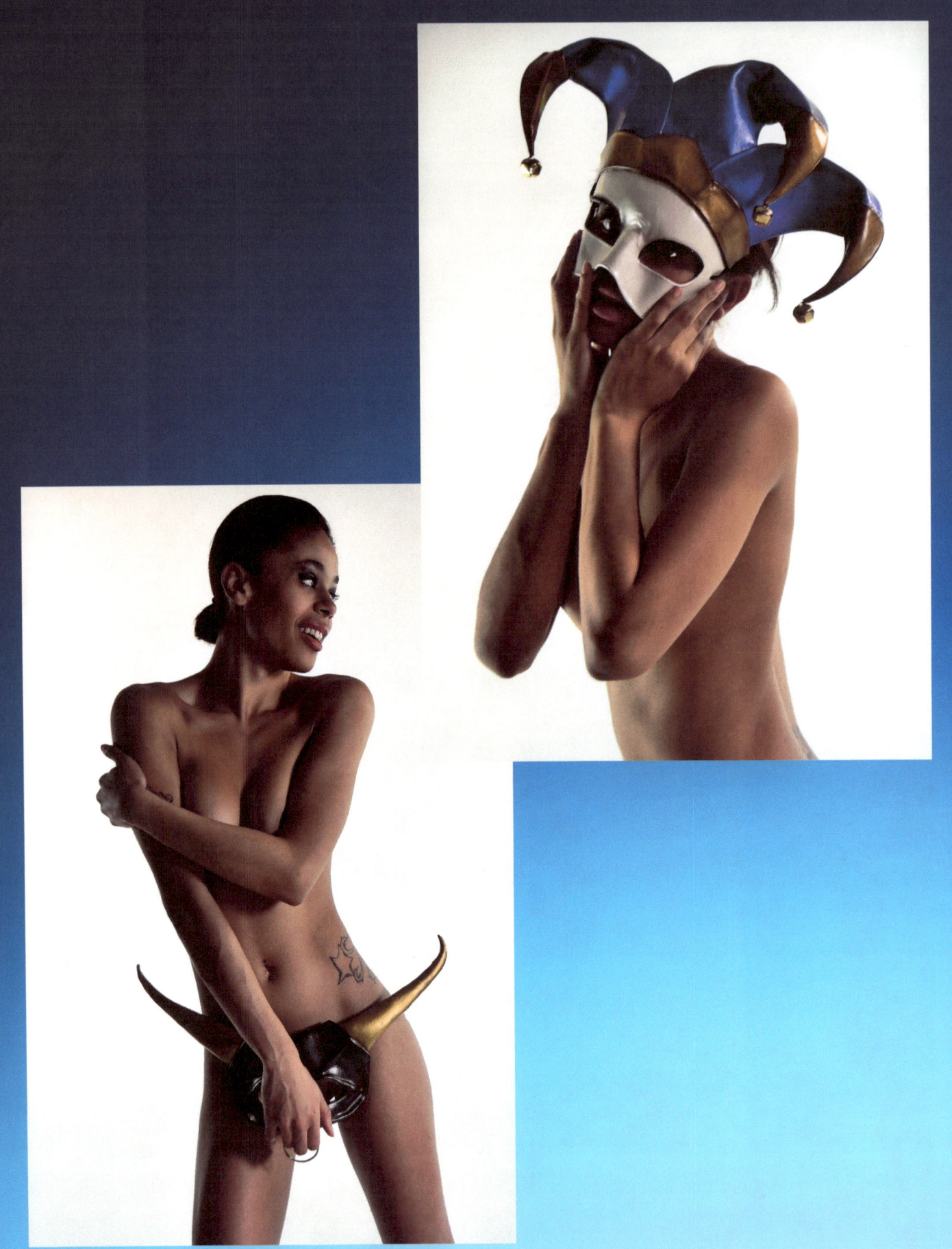

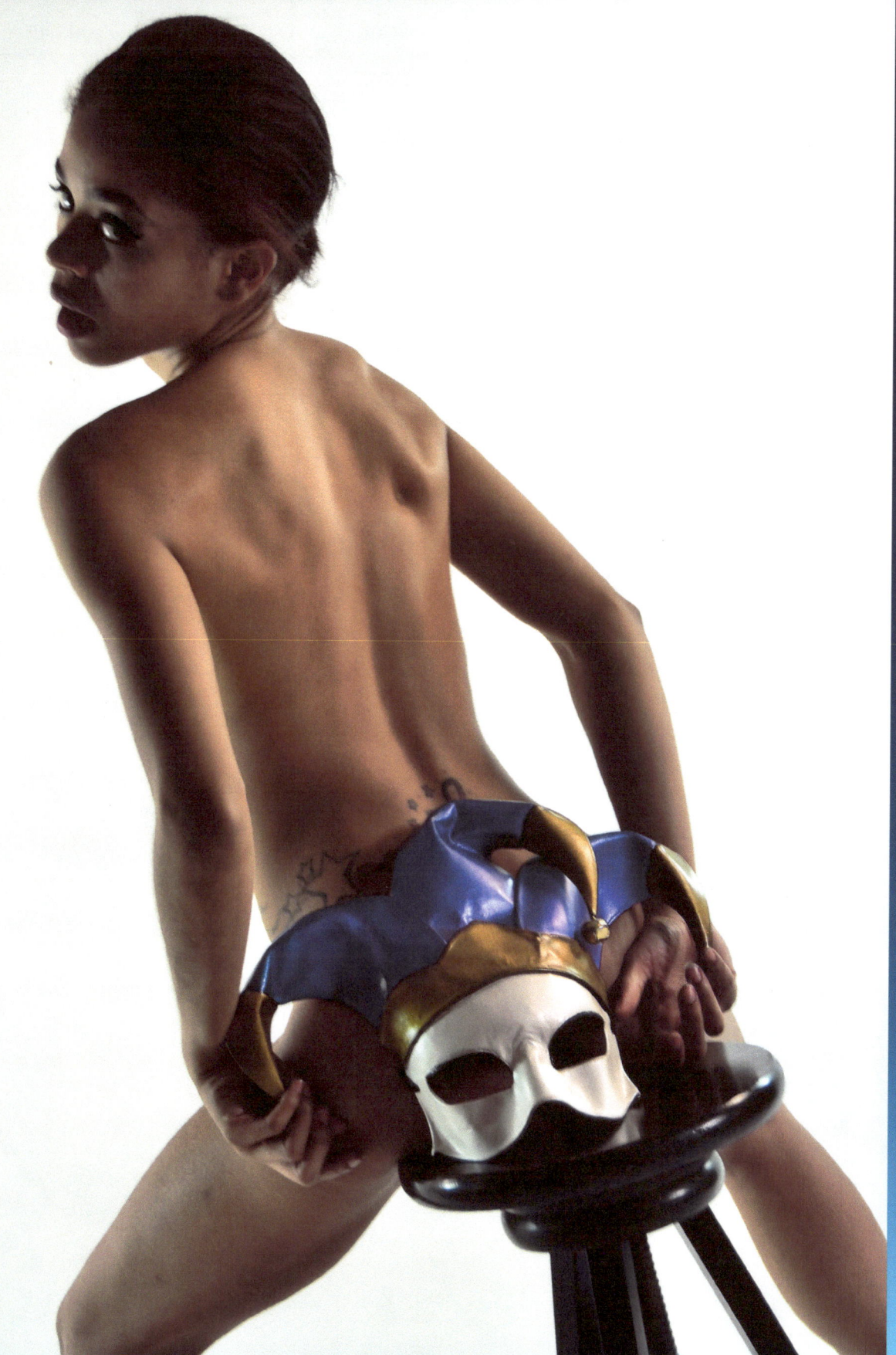

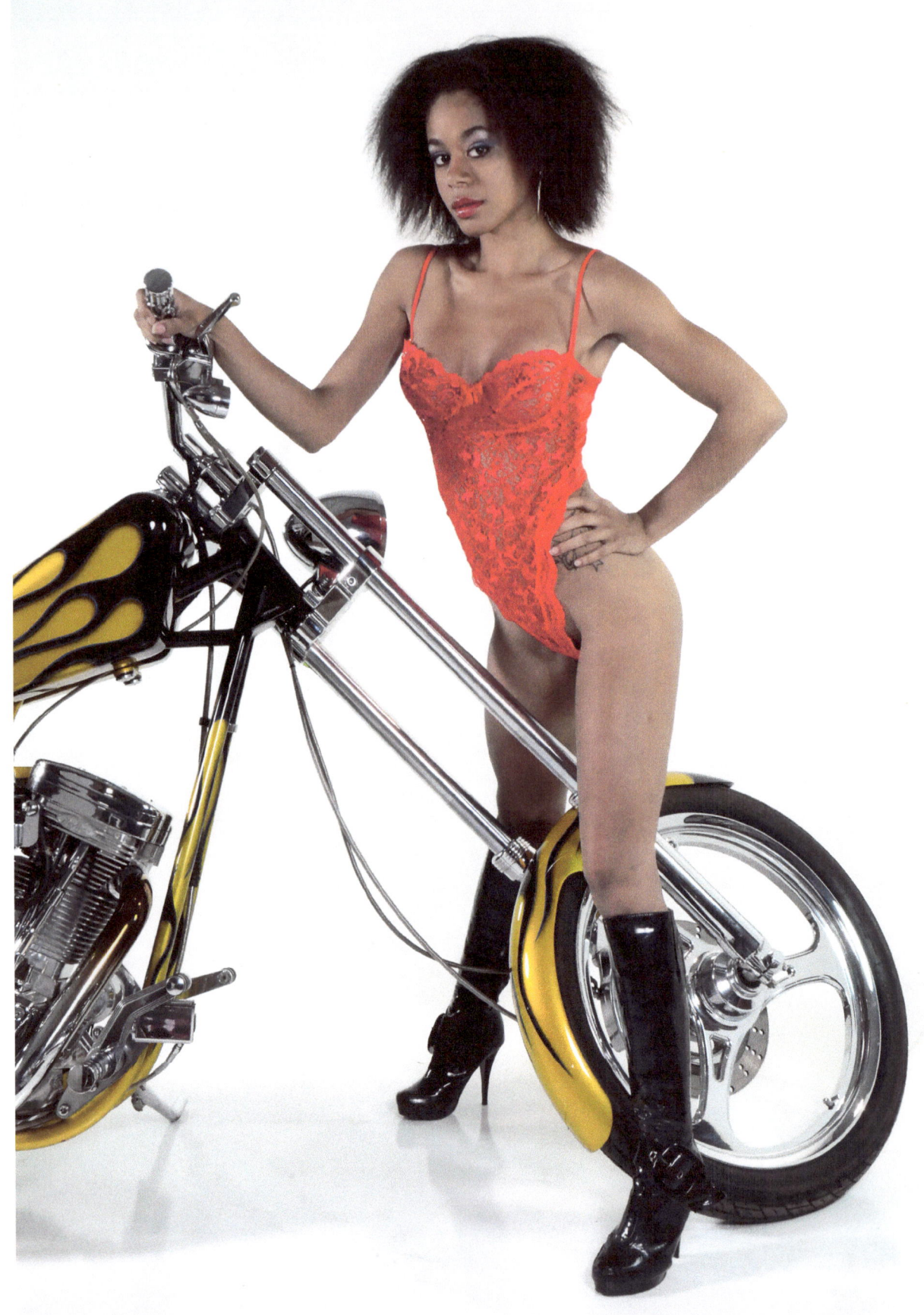

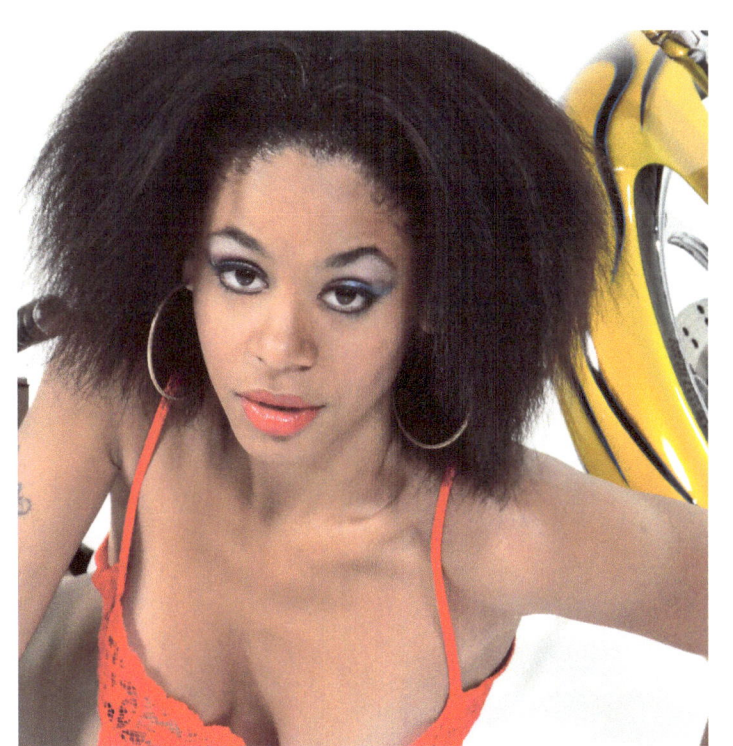

Beauty
and the
Bike

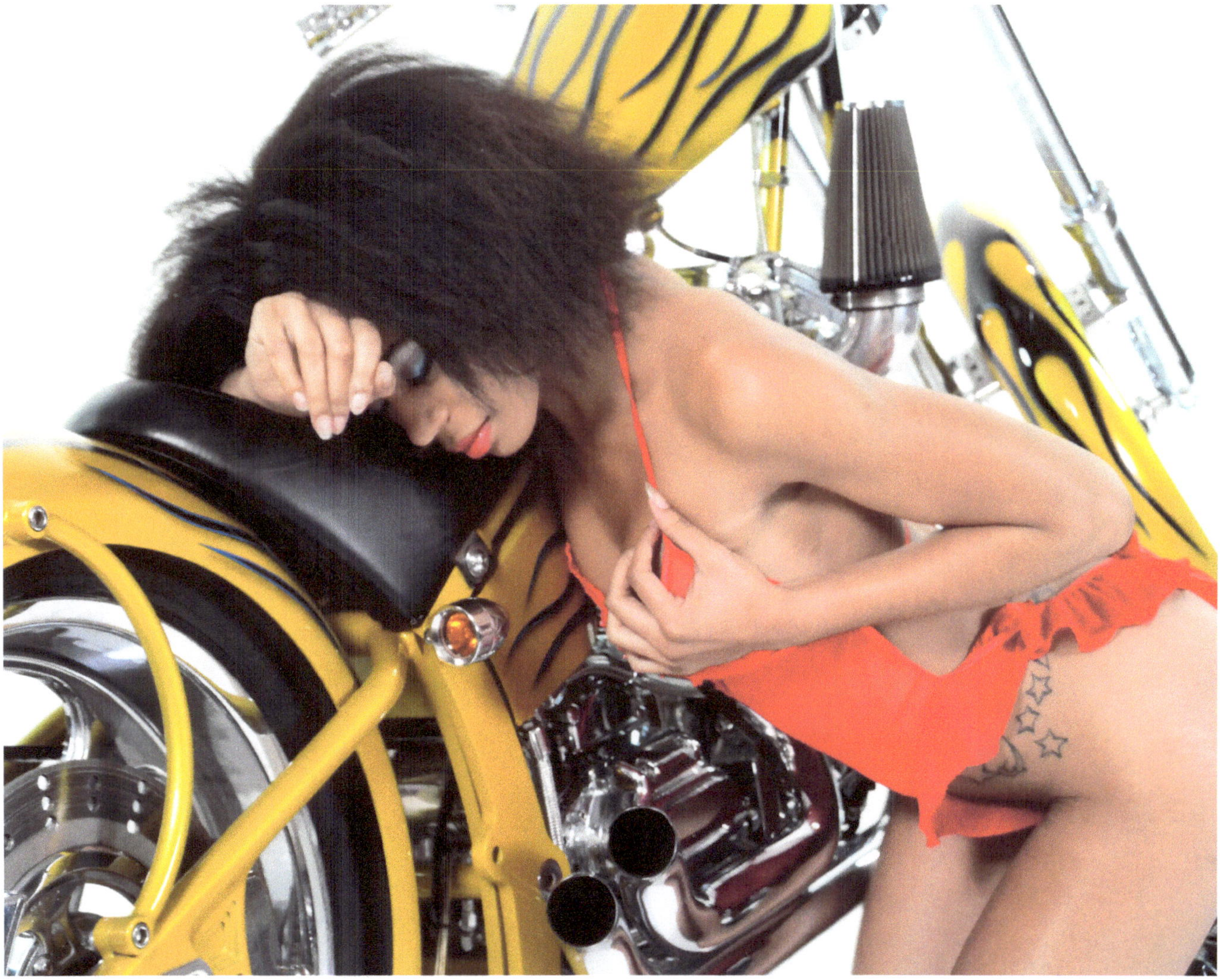

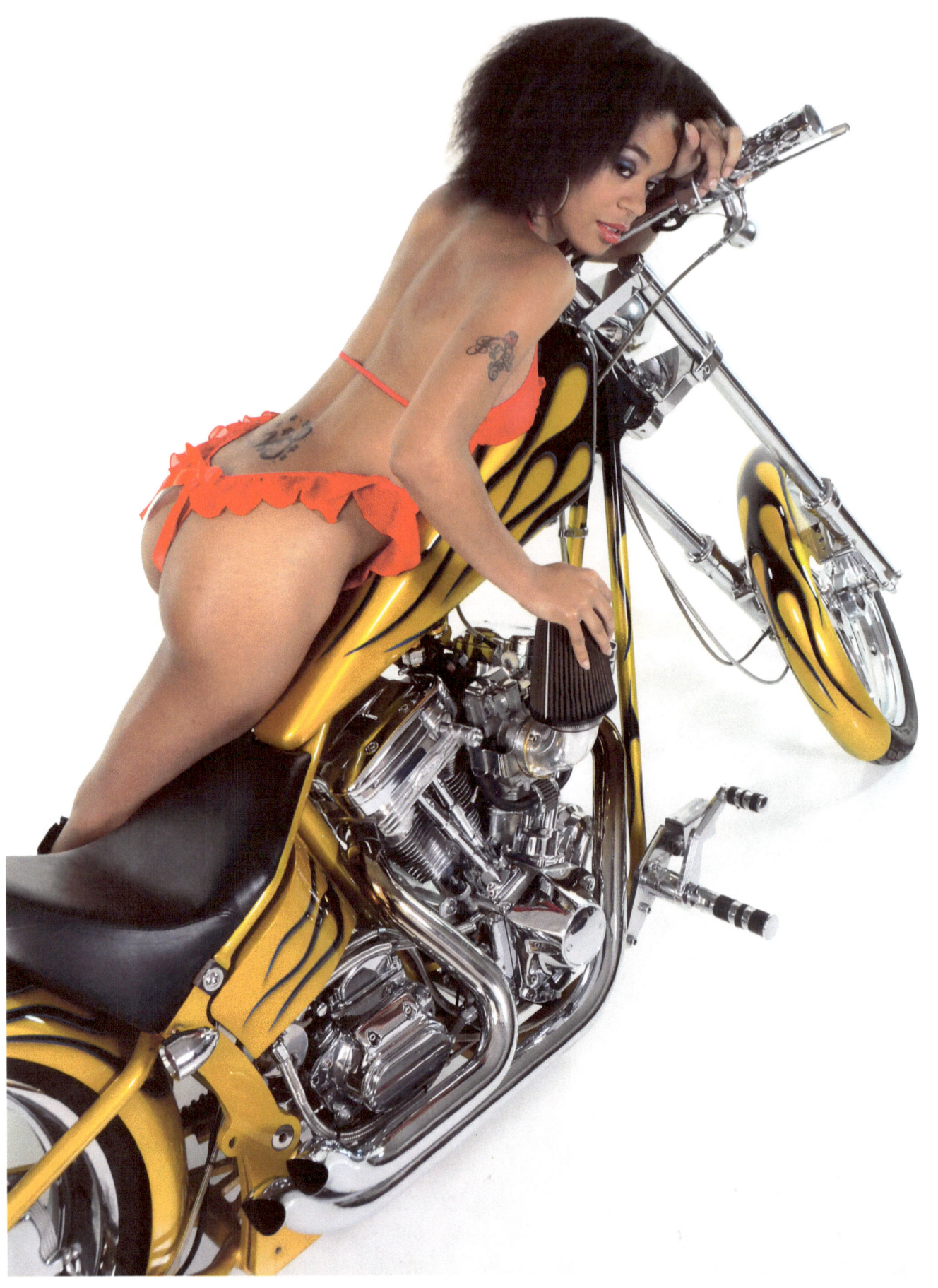

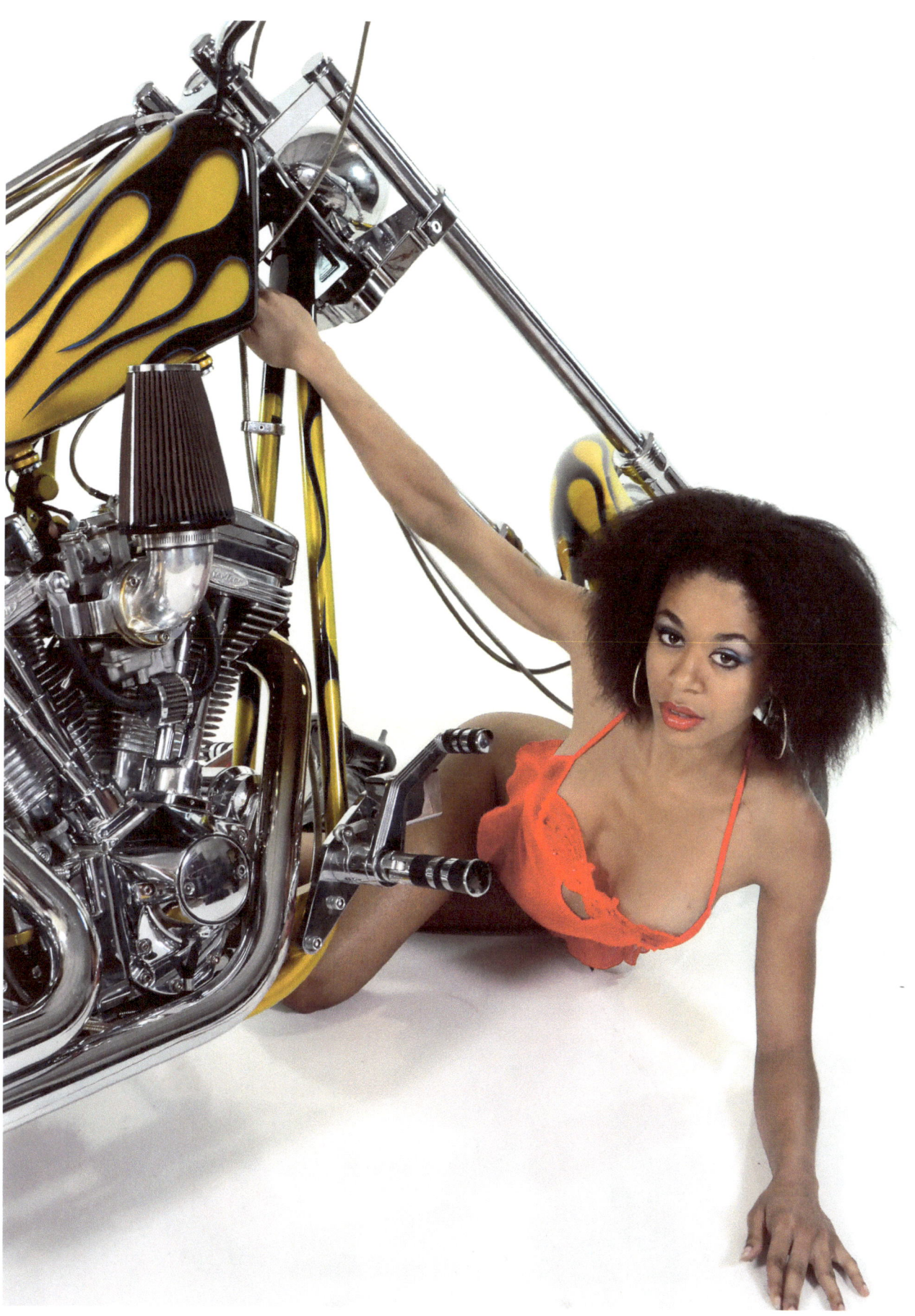

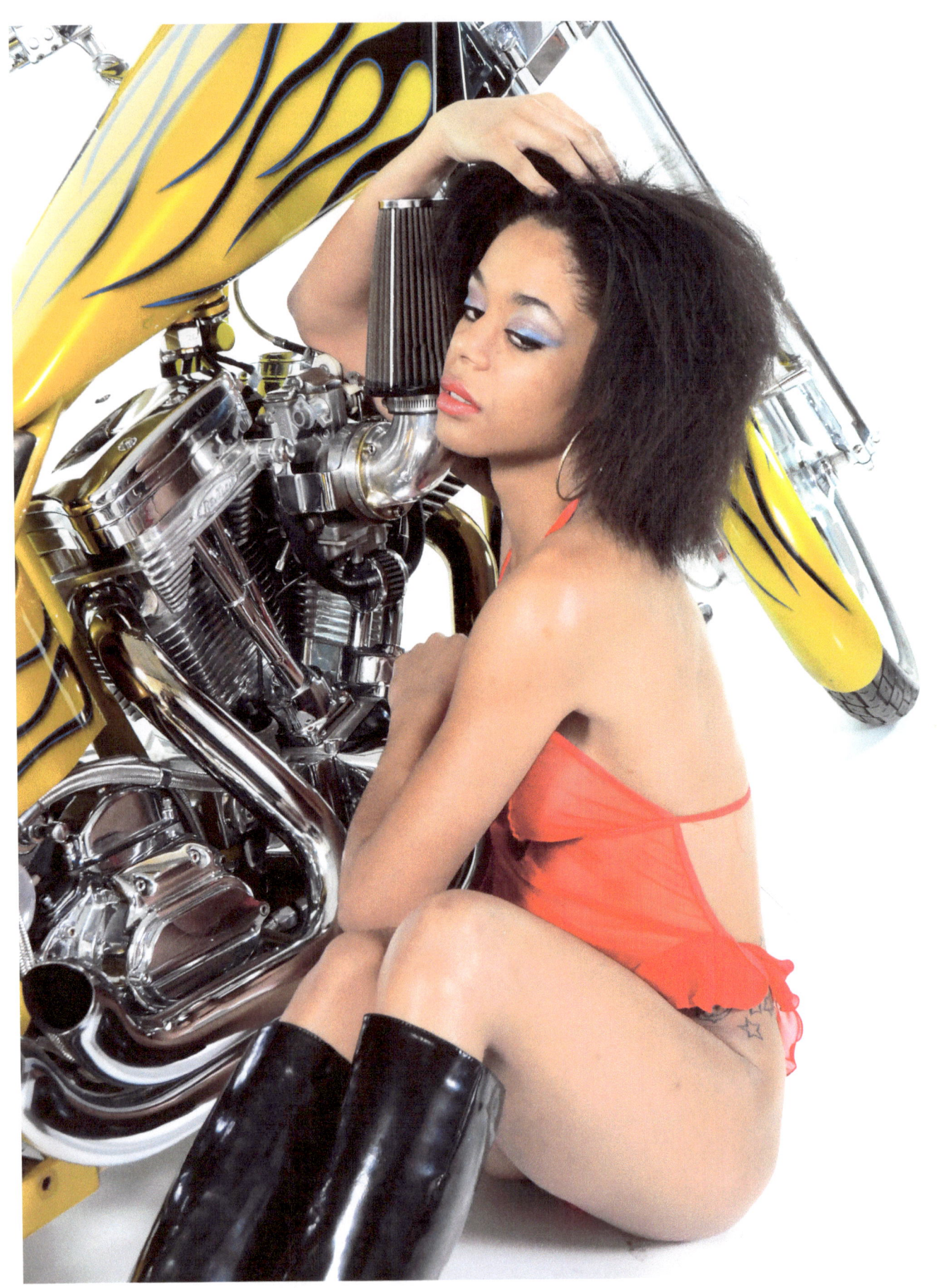

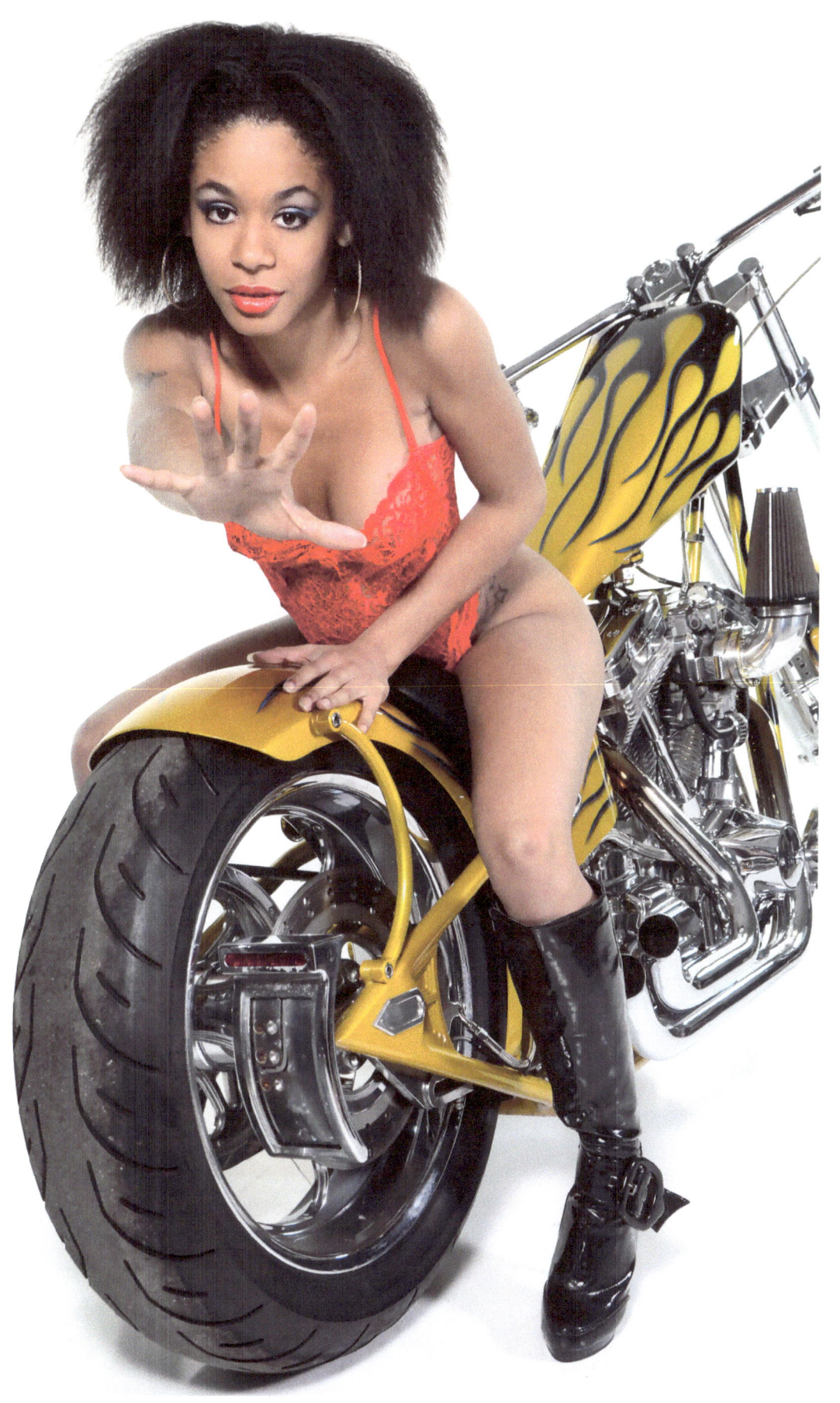

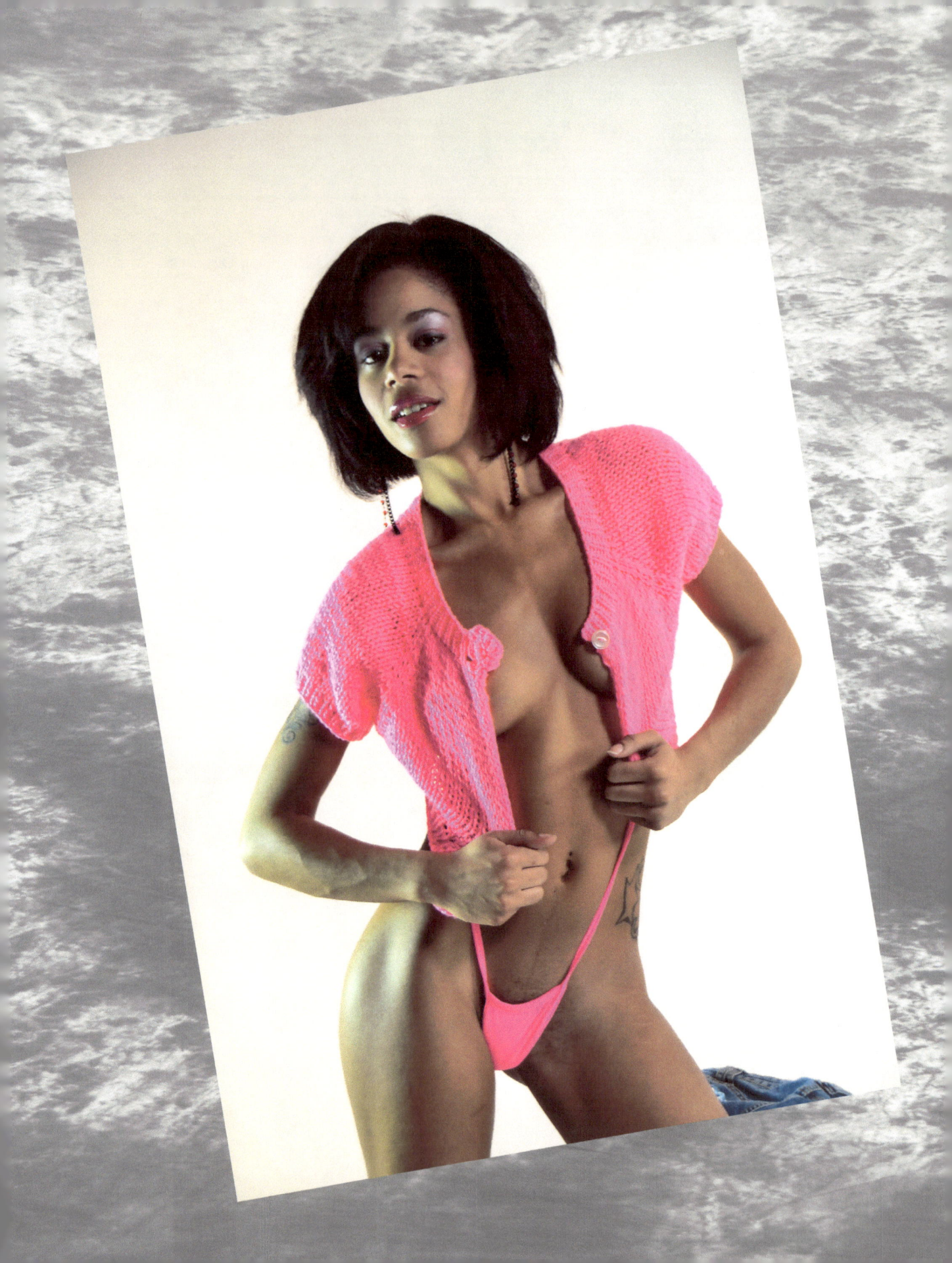

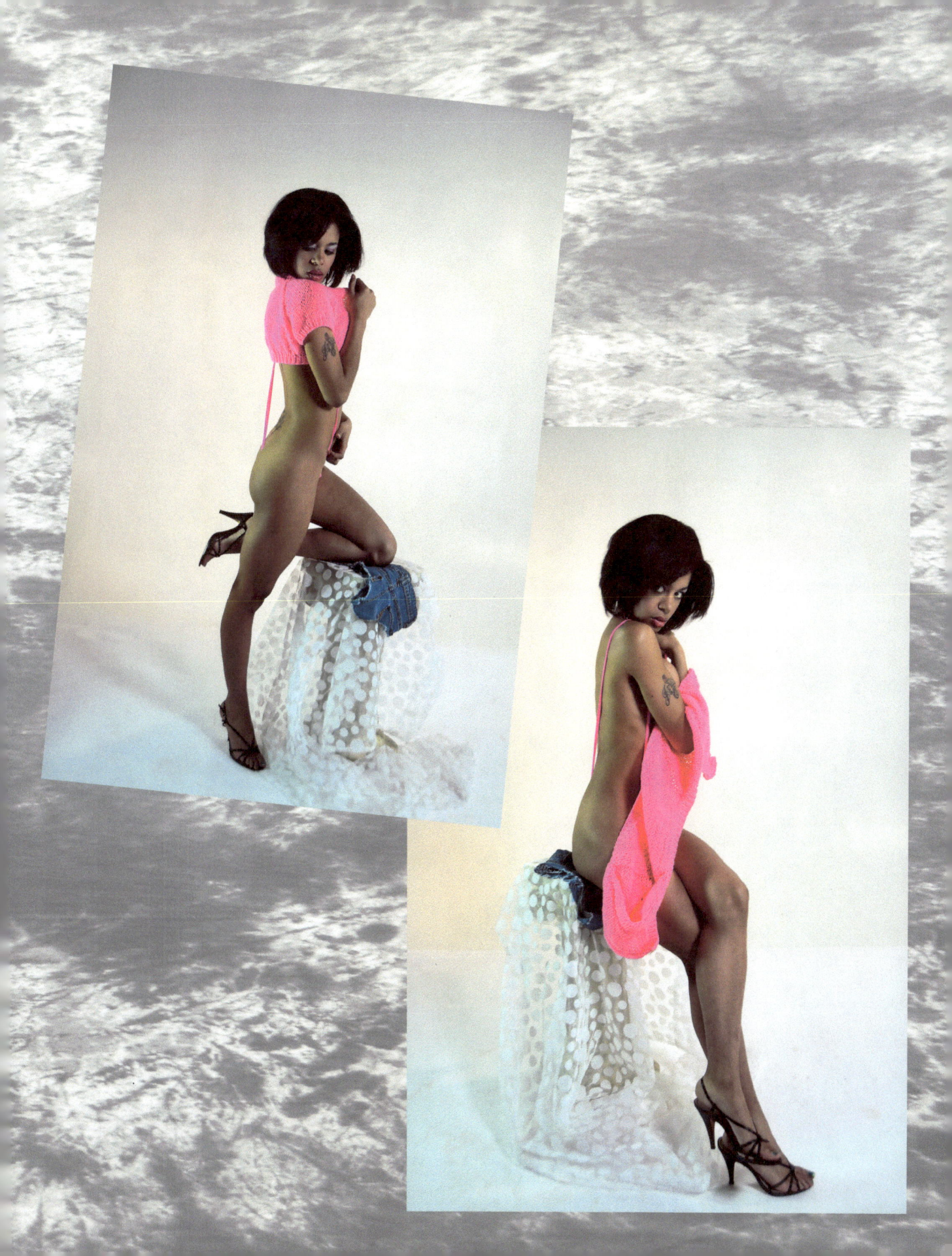

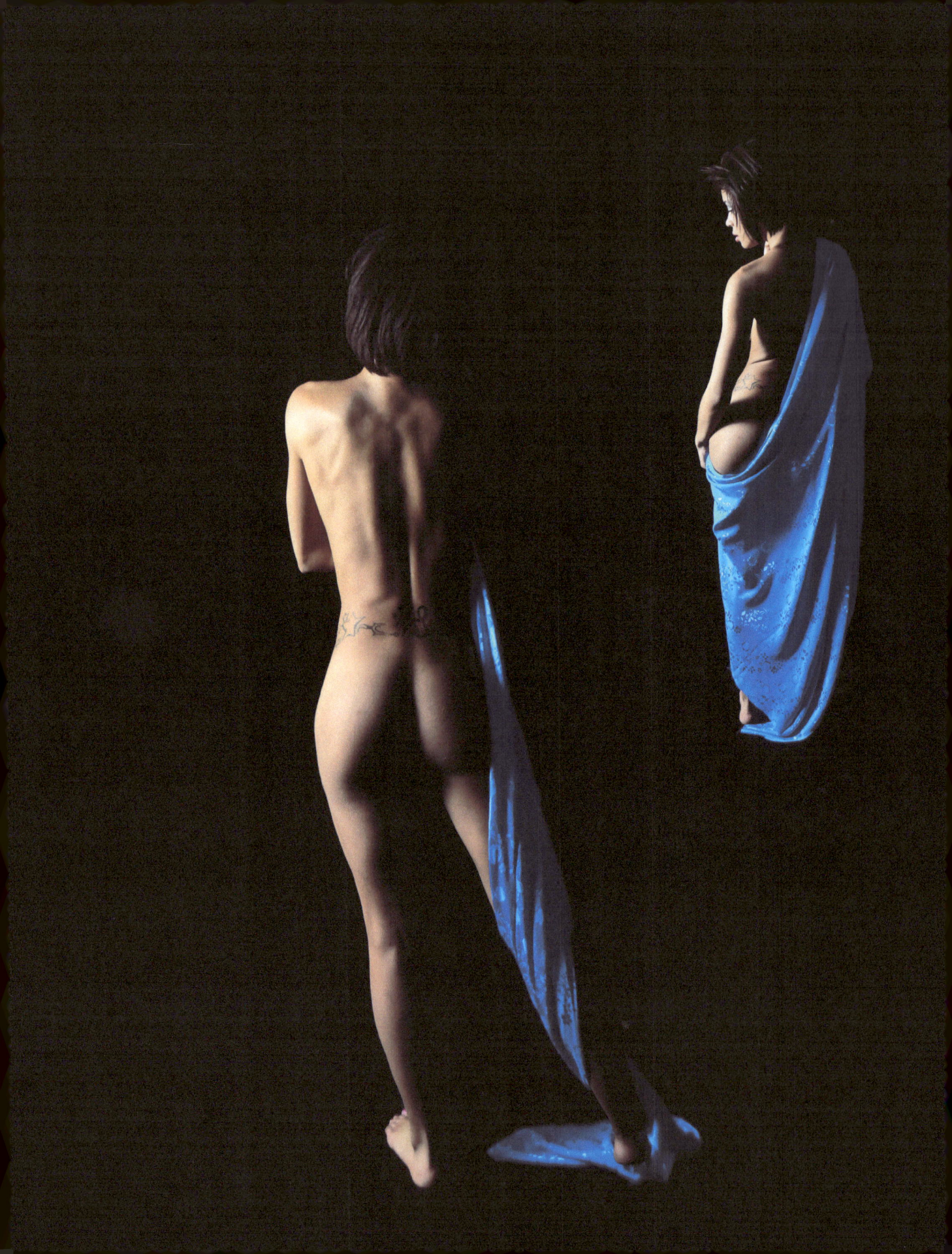

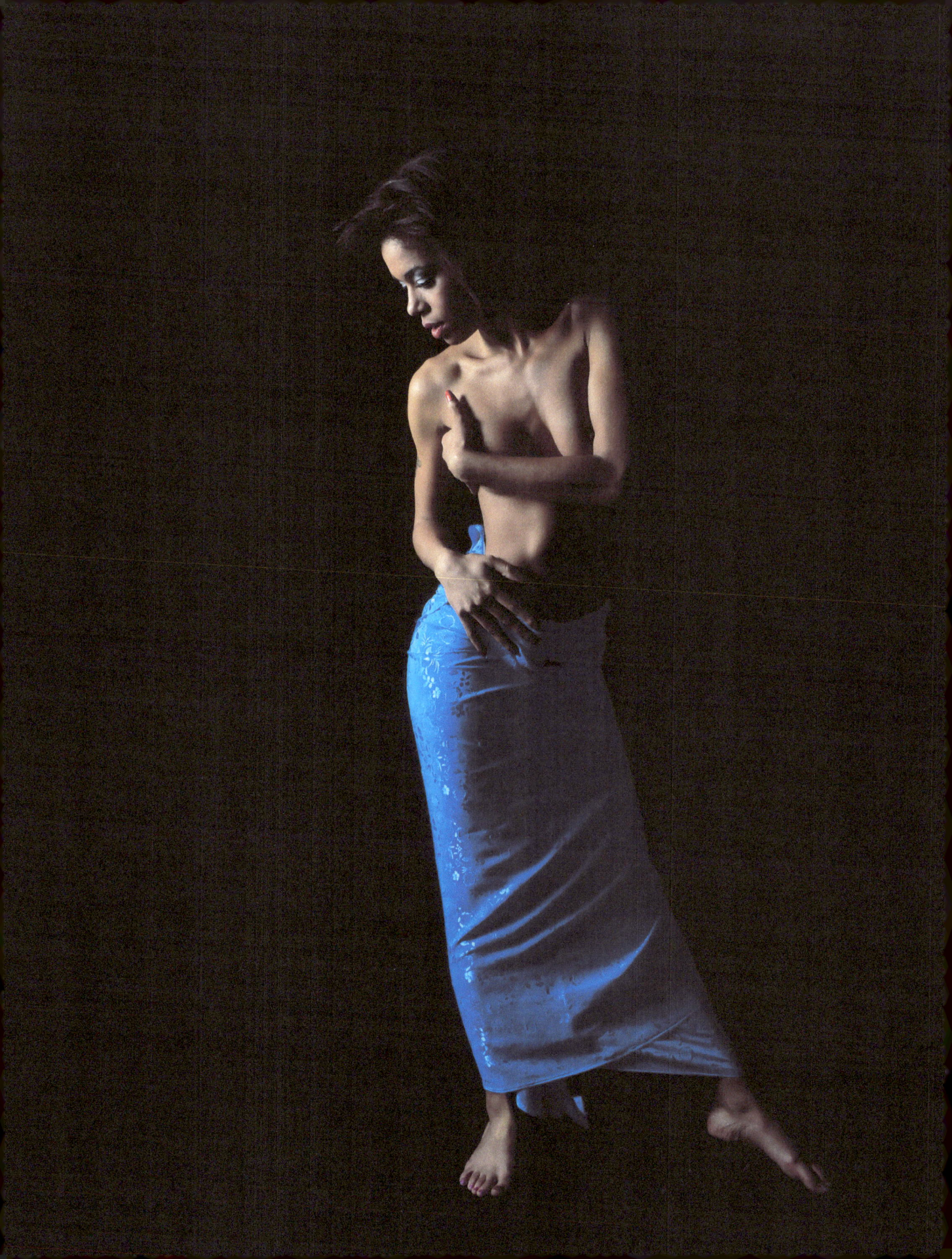

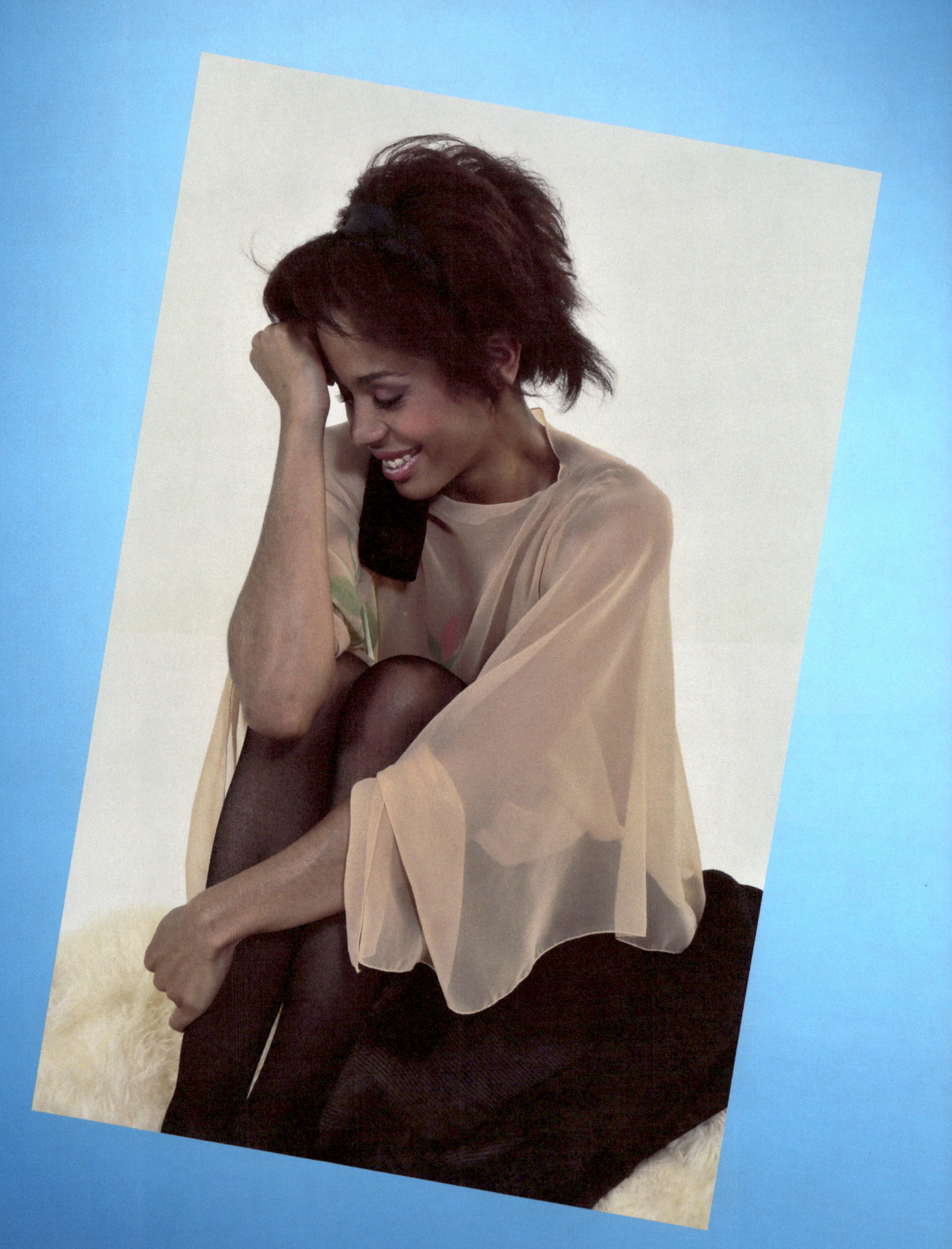

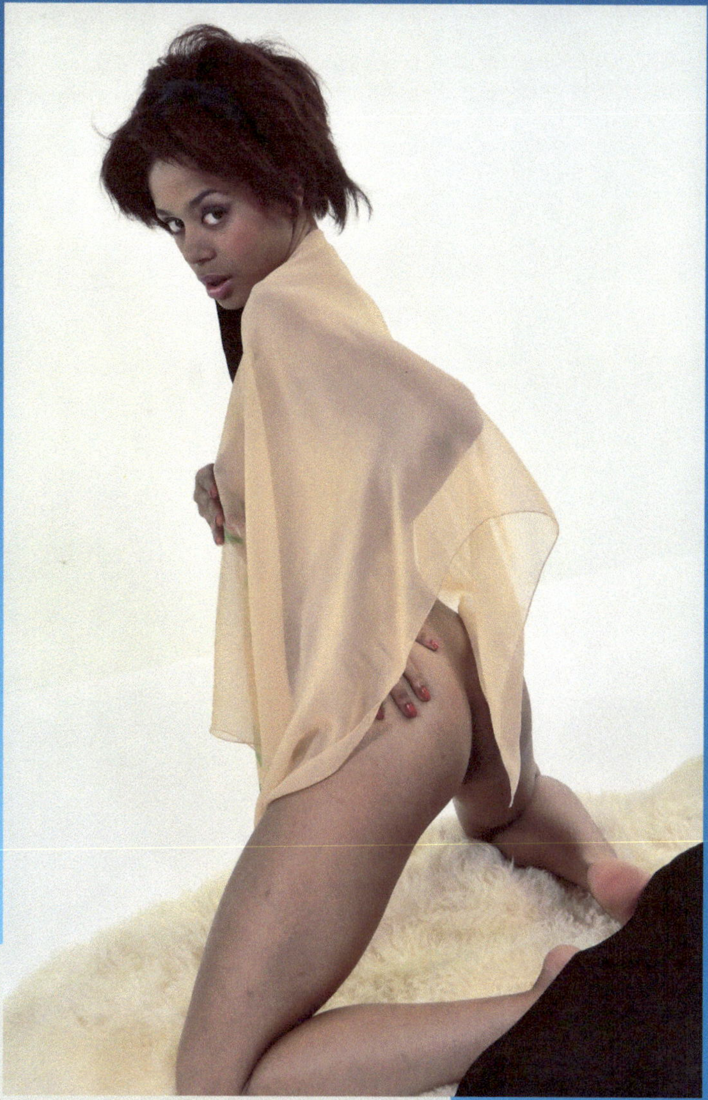

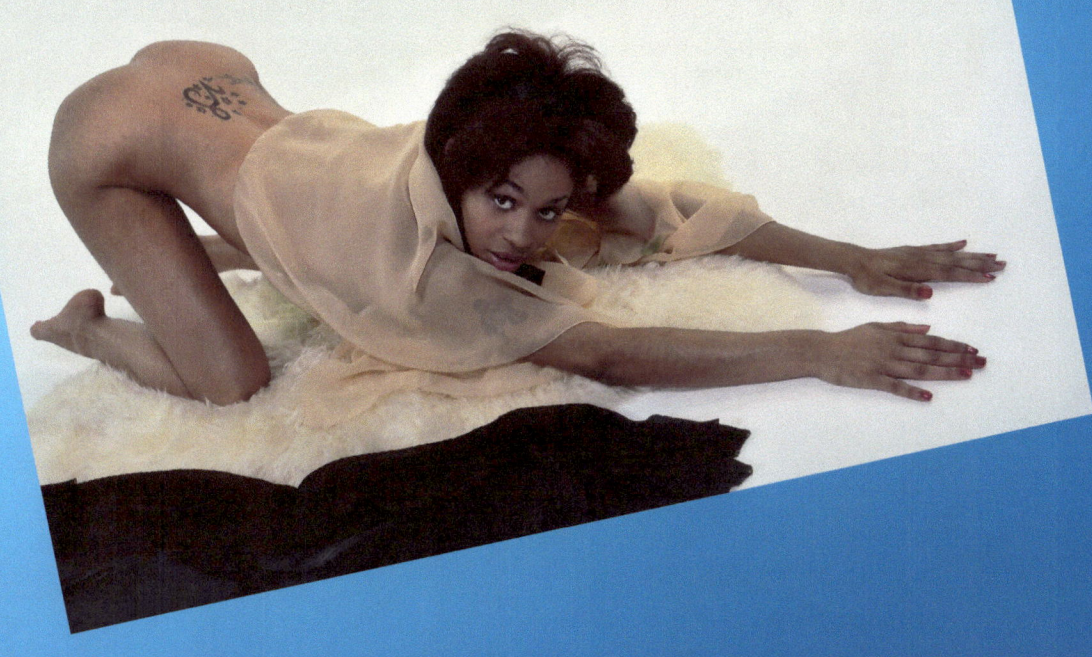

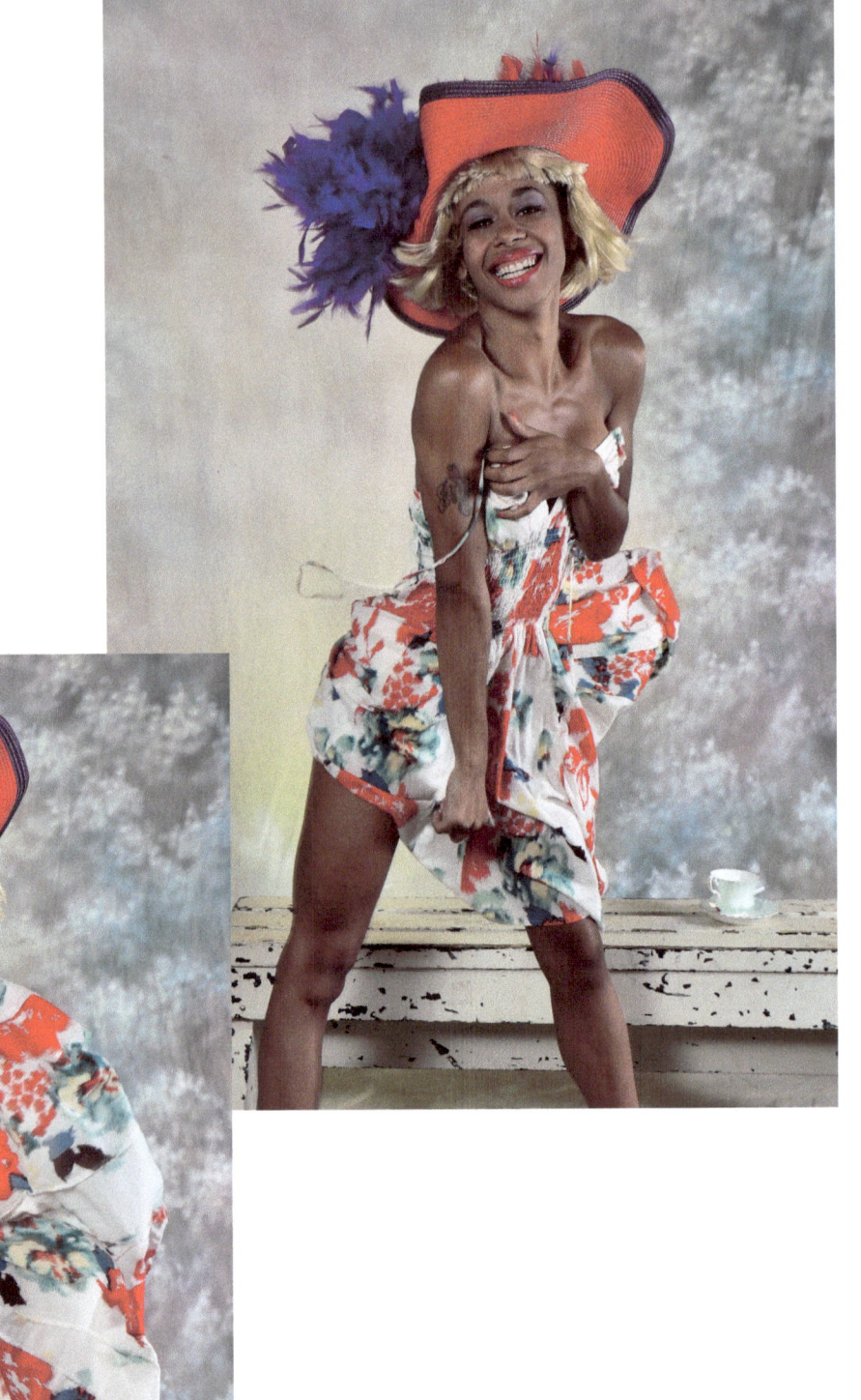

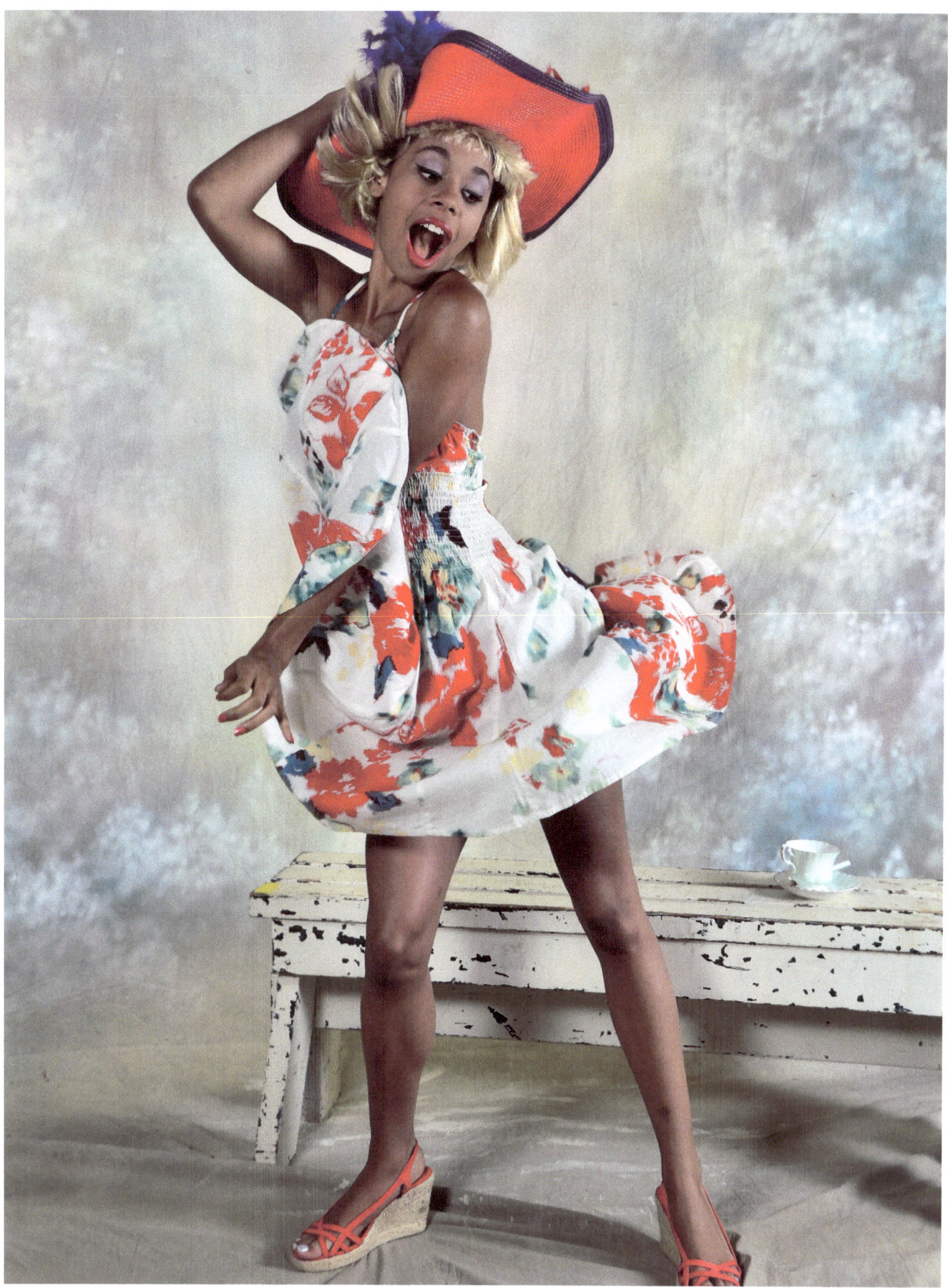

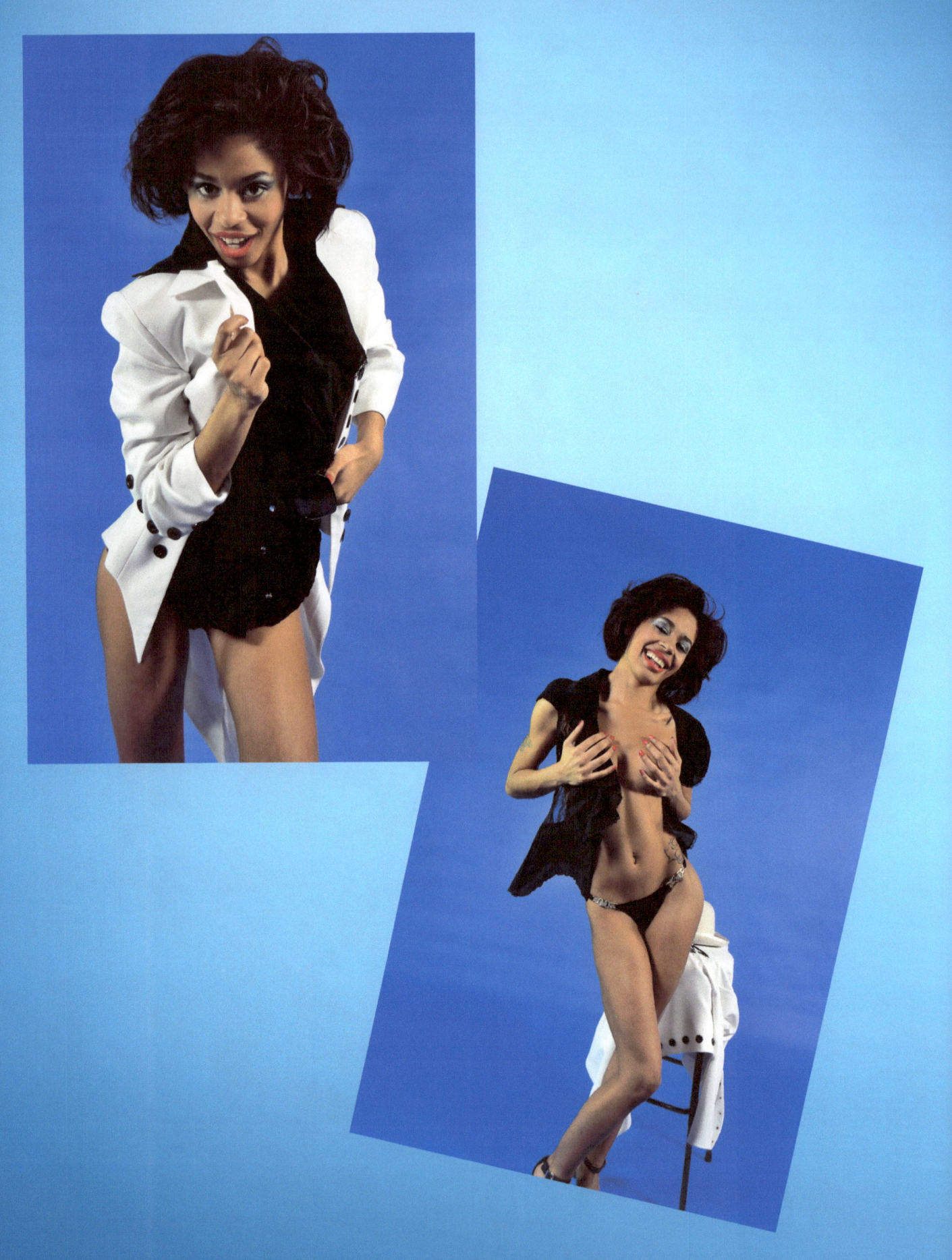

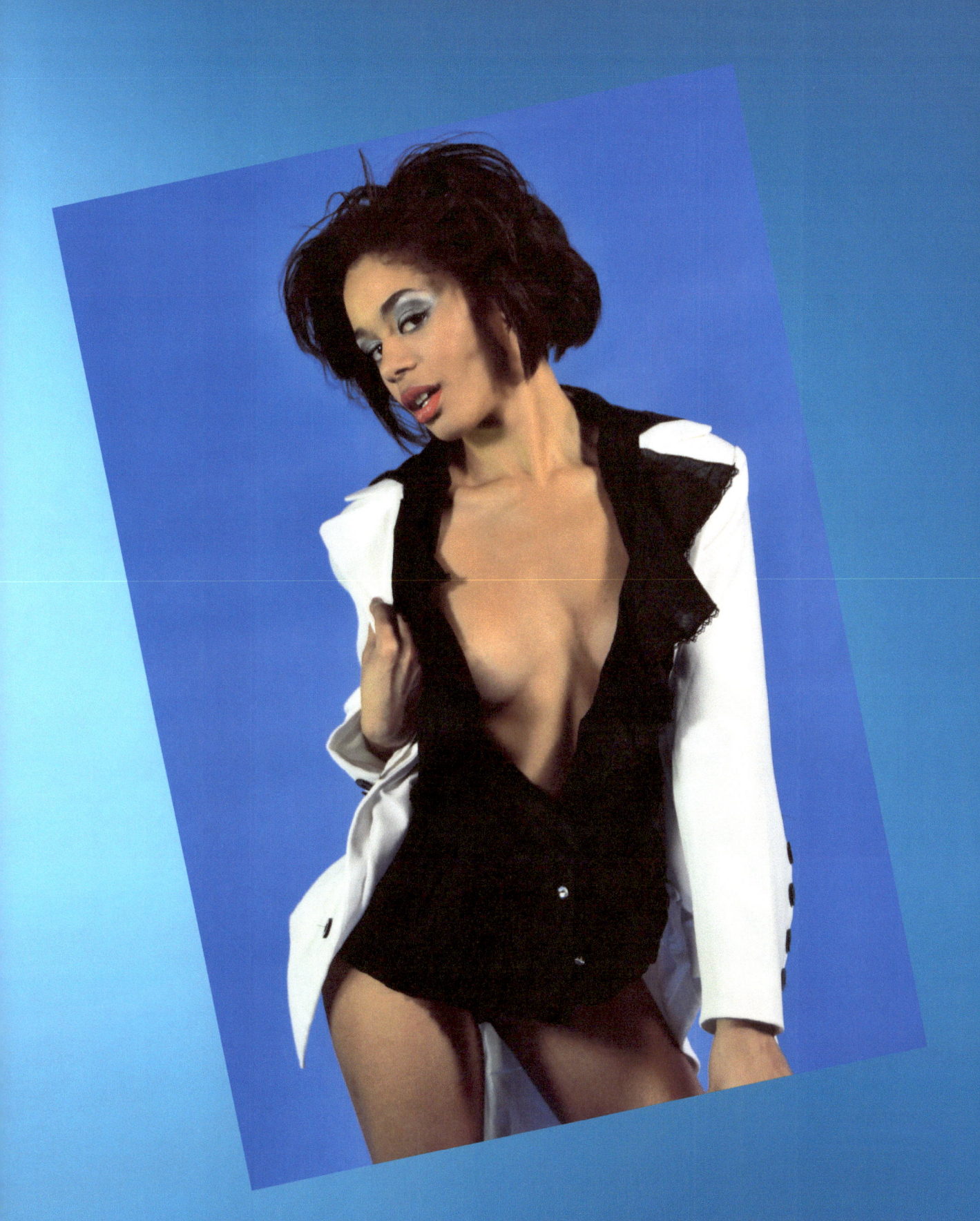

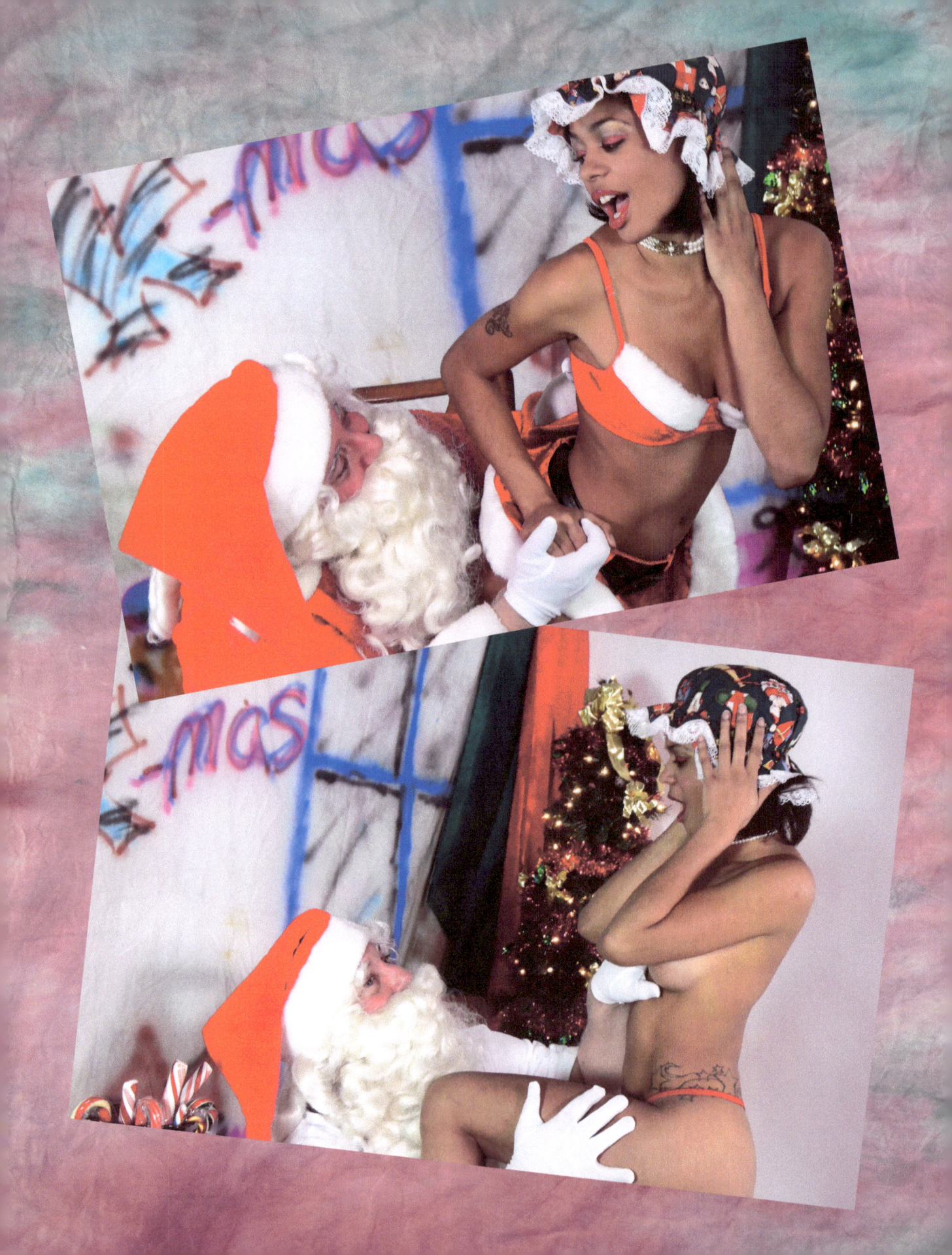

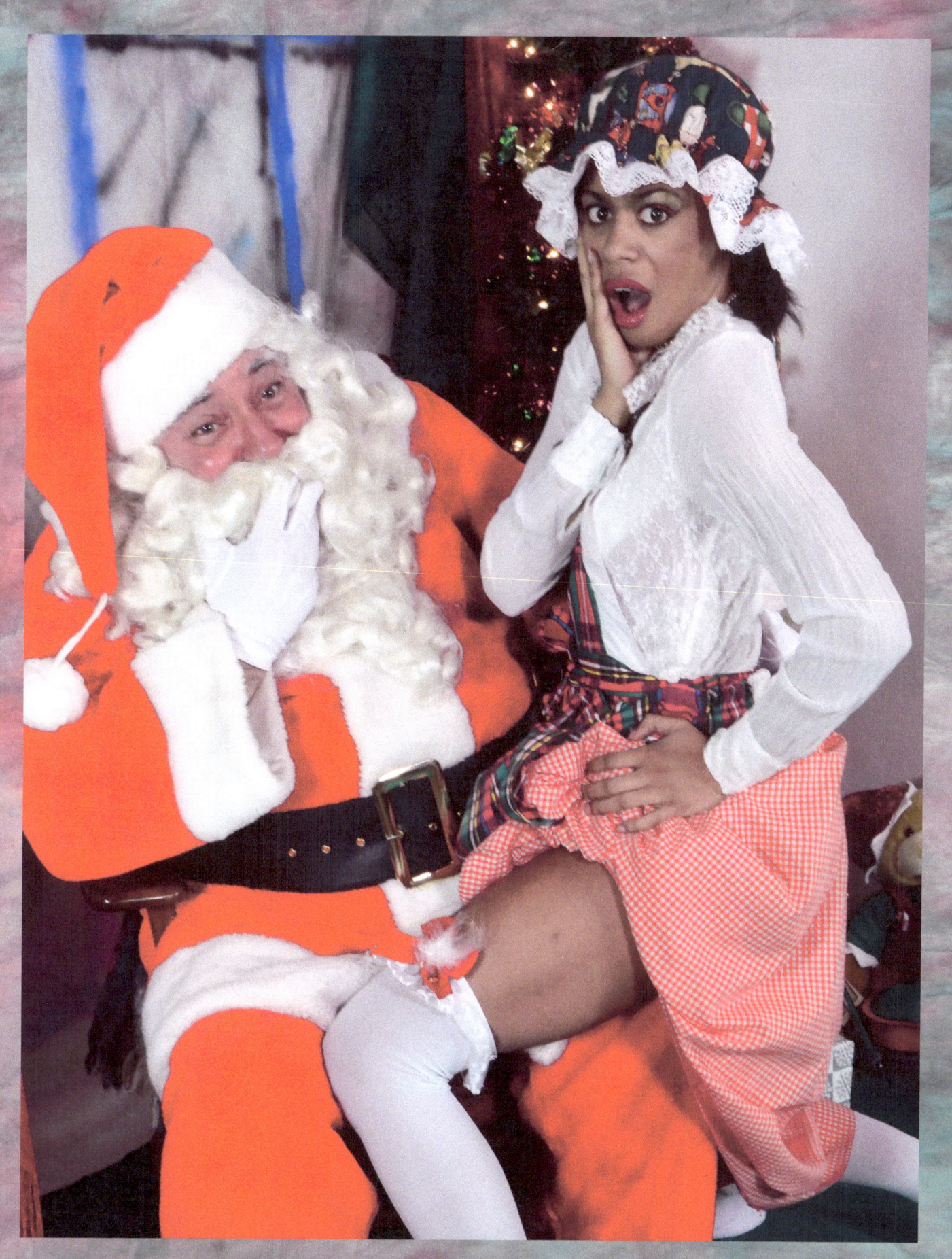

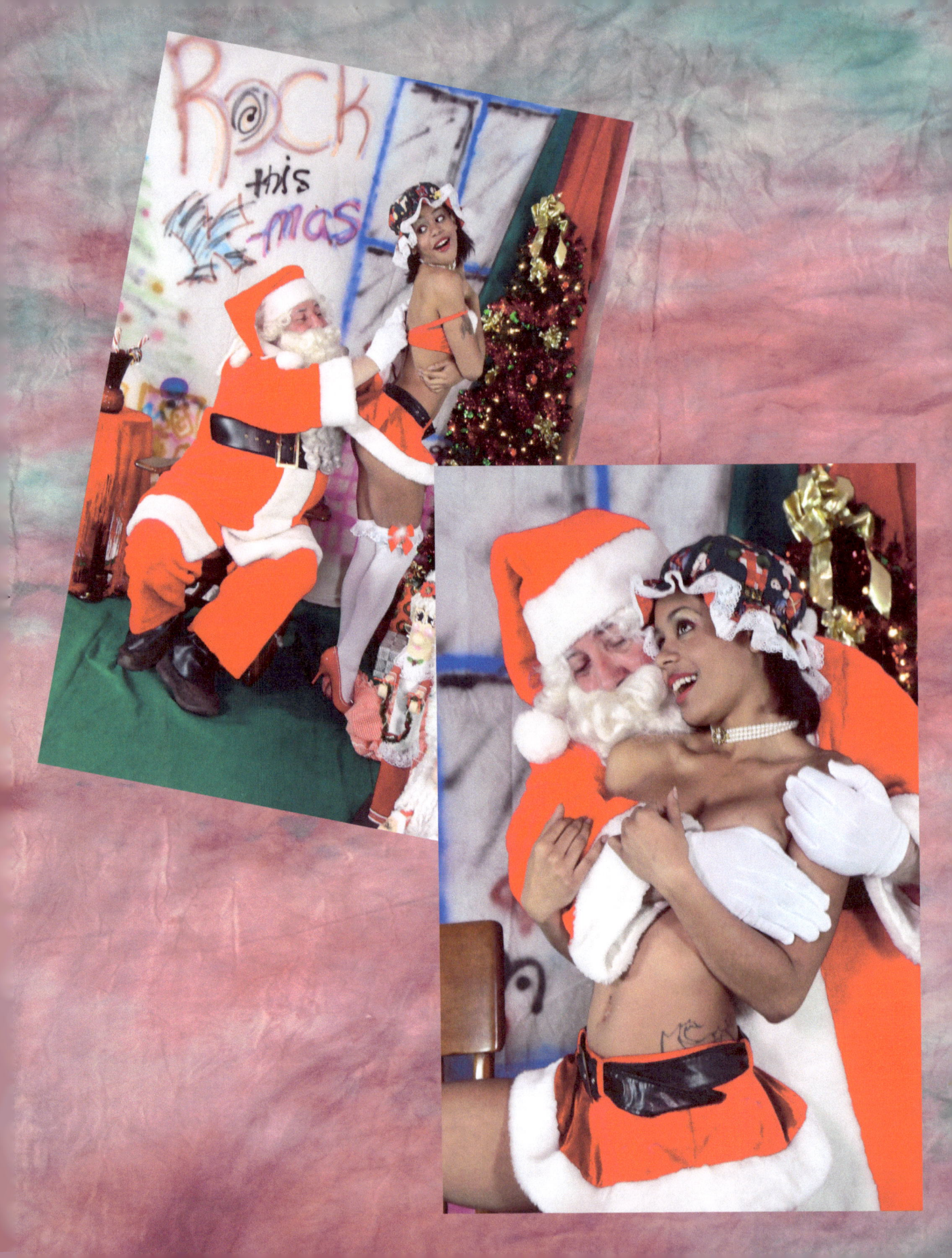

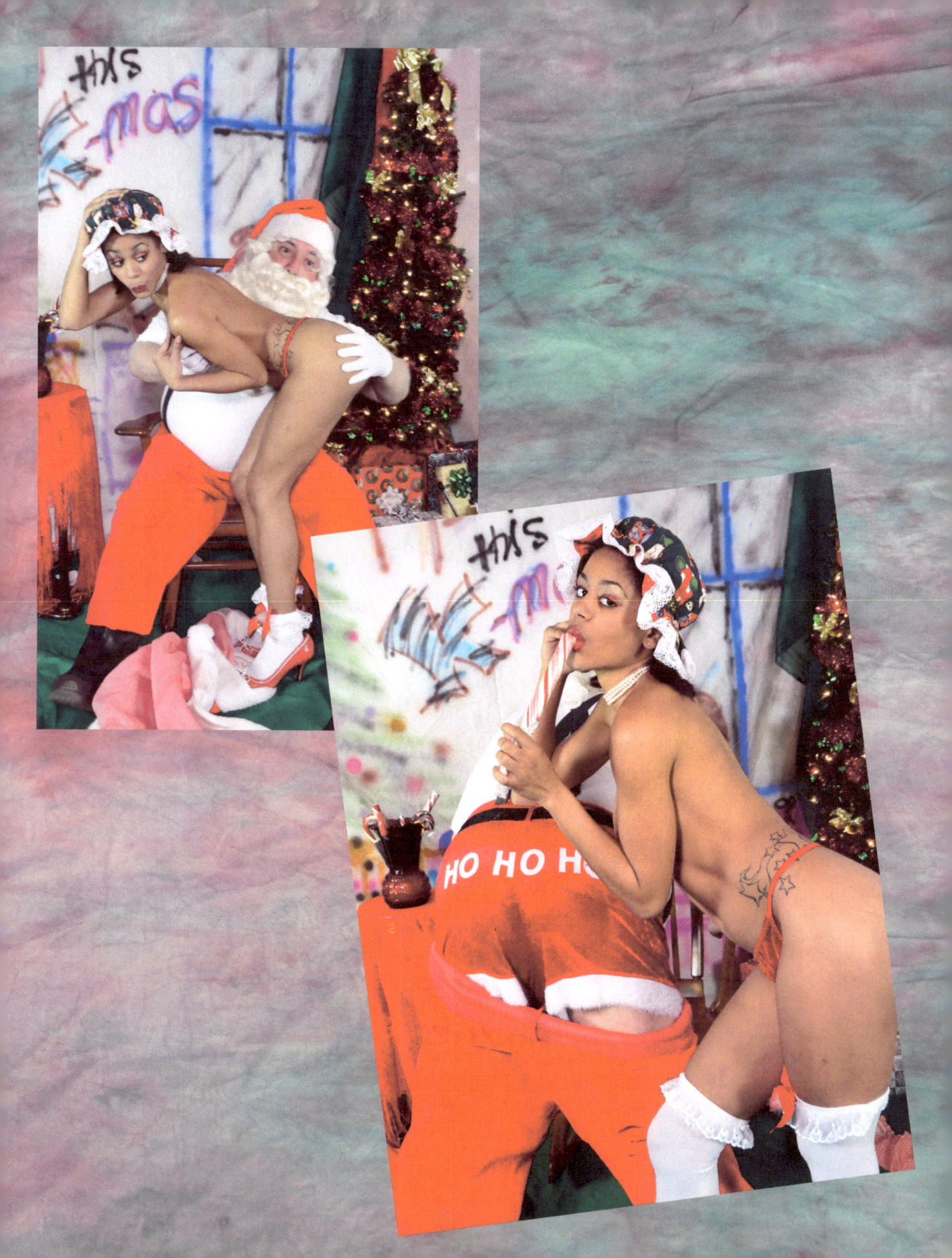

Available now in Hardback
Coffee Table Edition from :

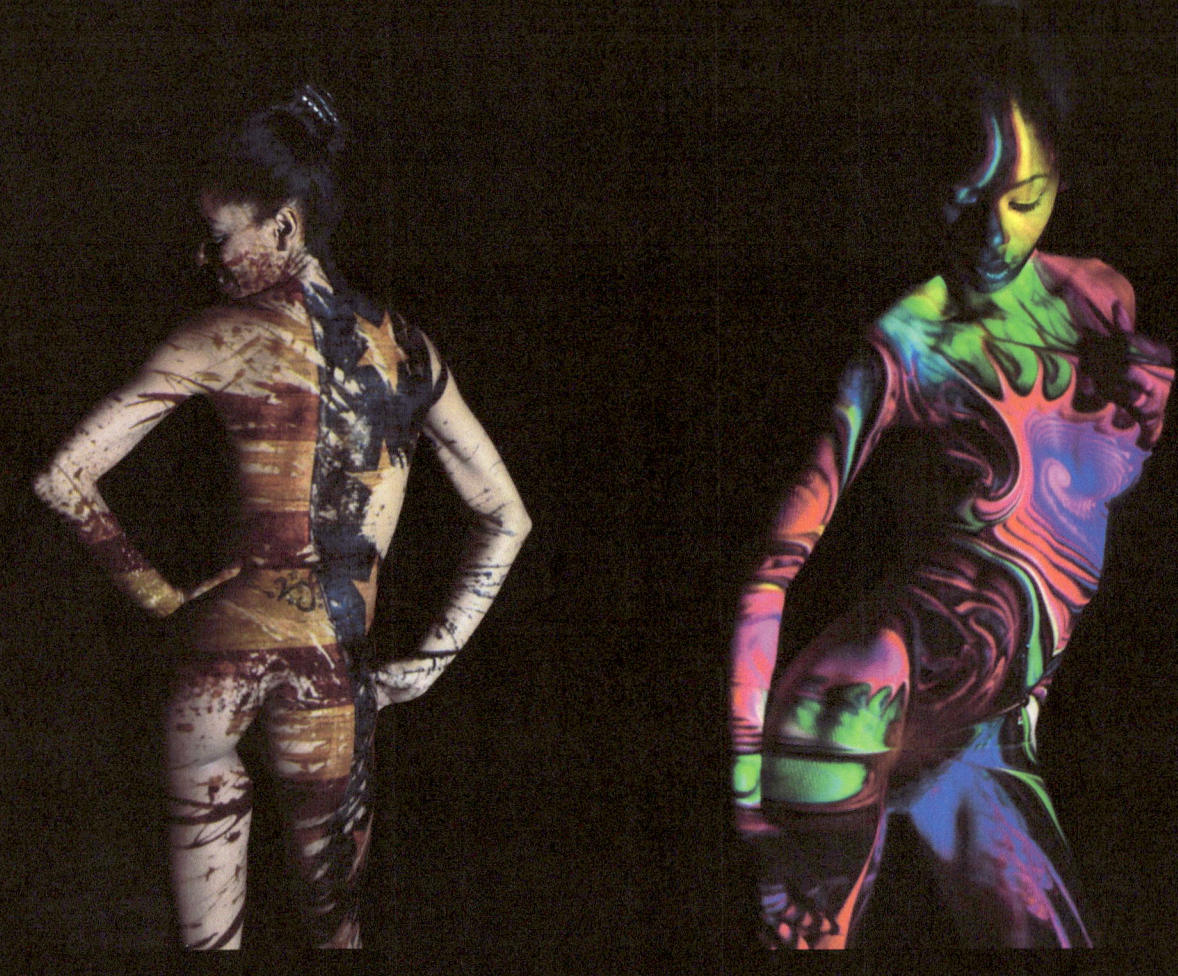

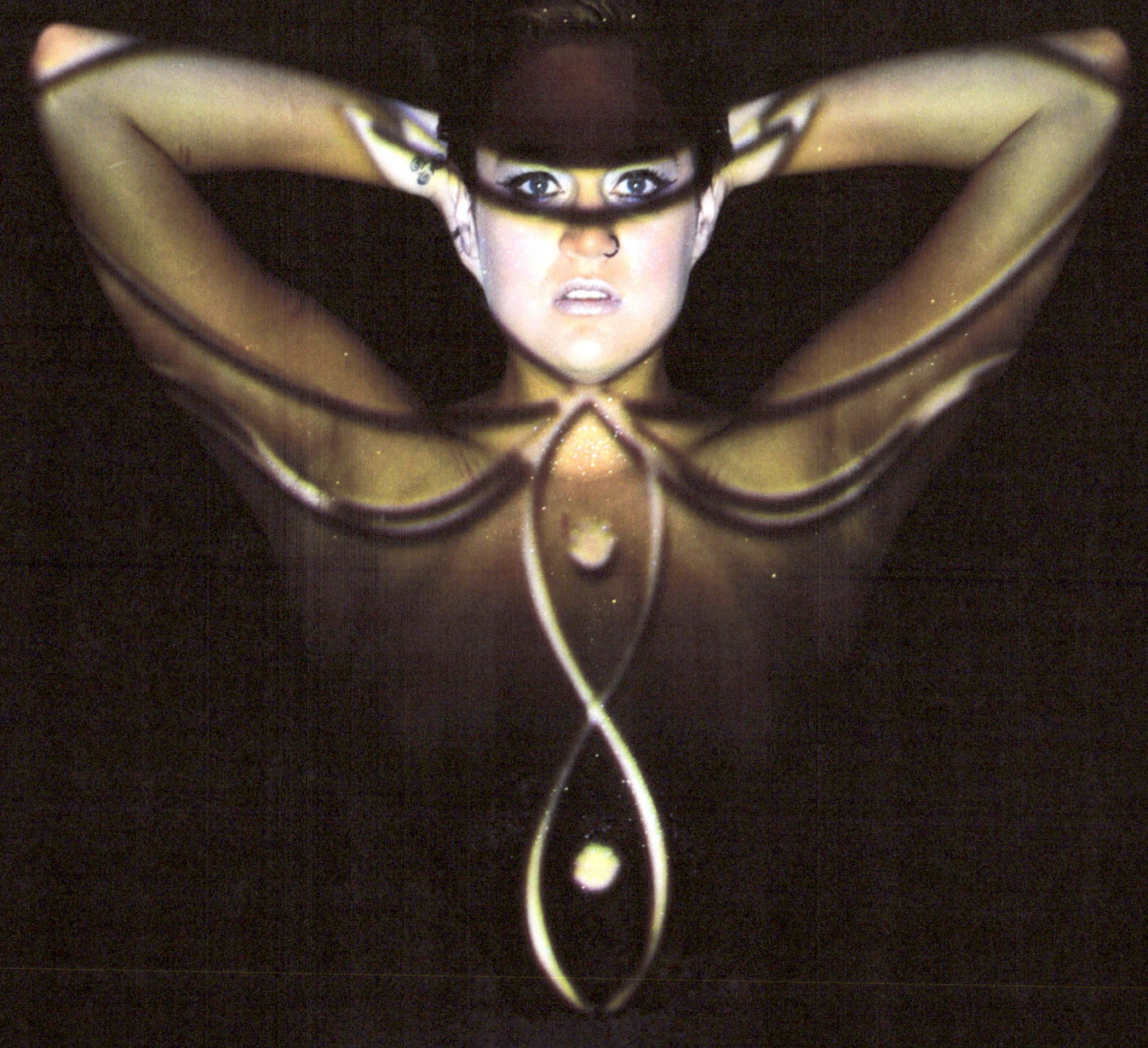

Naked in the Light

By Leighty and Tormen

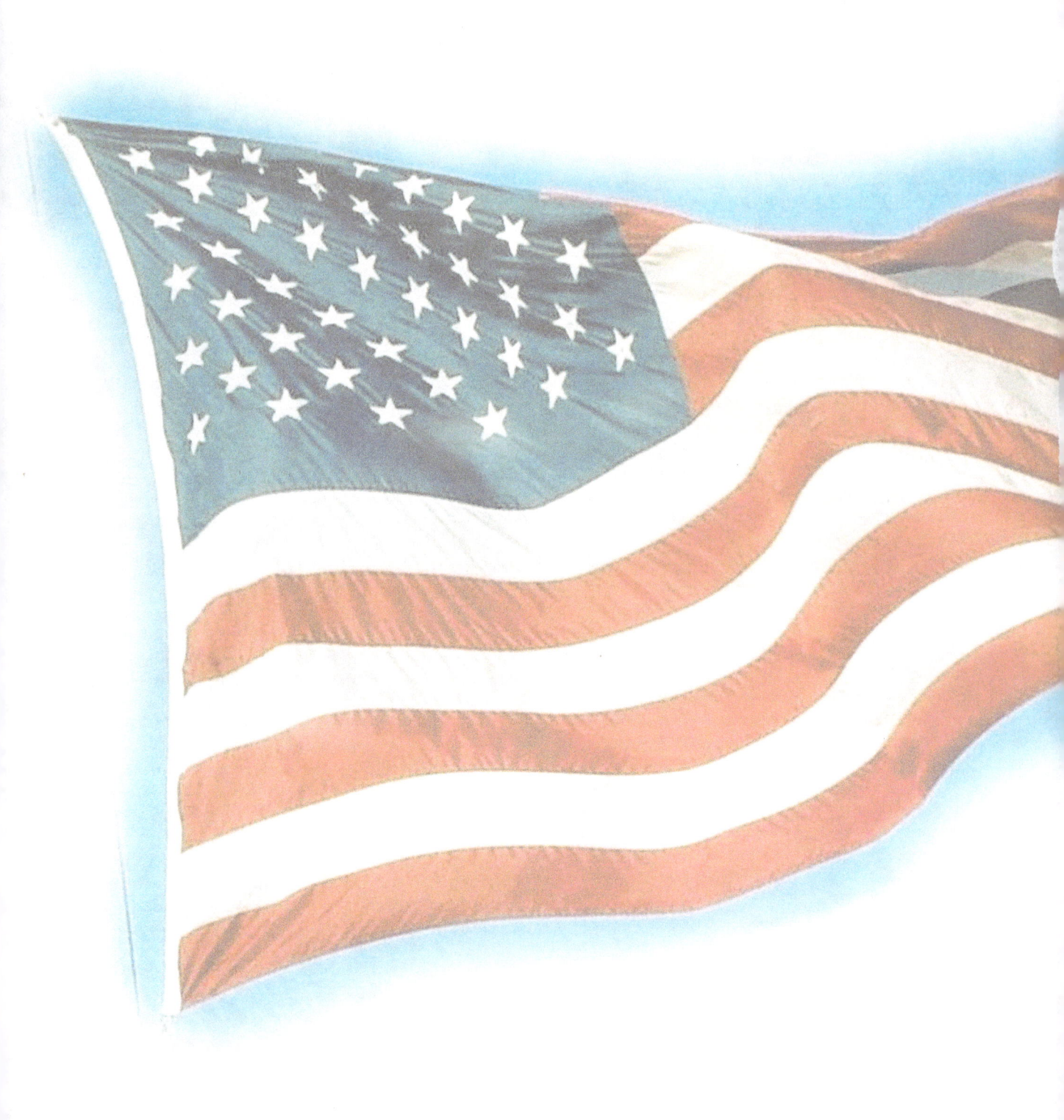

Mark Leighty

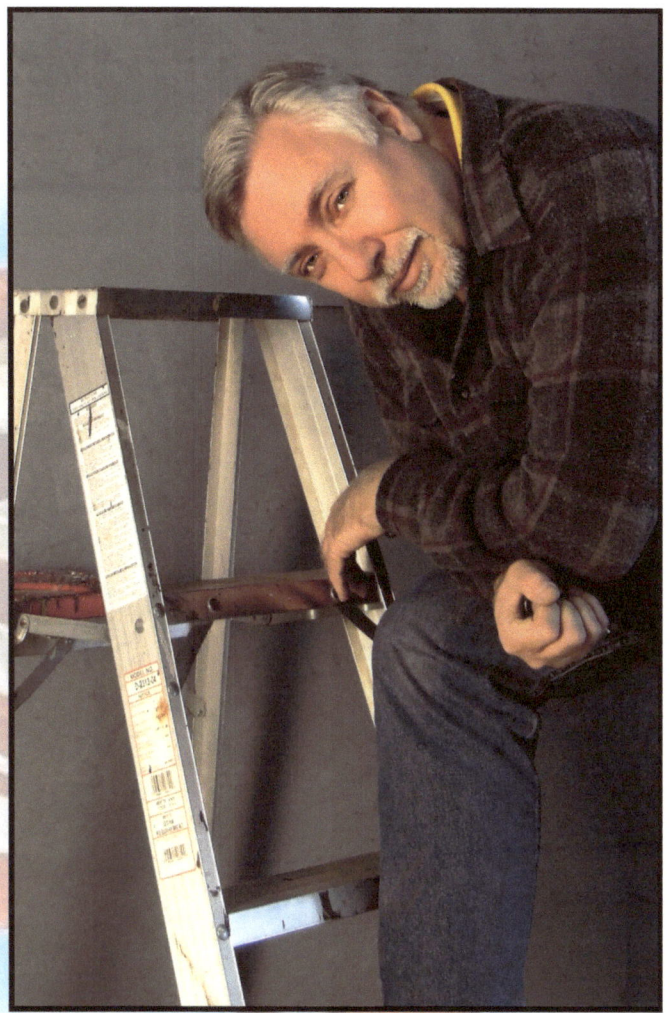

Mark Leighty is a not so typical middle-class American. A Baby-Boomer of the 50's, he attended military school during the Vietnam War and received an appointment to the US Naval Academy, but instead chose to attend a small college in the North-West region of PA

He has worked as busboy, bellhop and amusement park employee. then later became machinist welder, electrical / electronics and pneumatics / hydraulics industrial designer and fabricator. He is currently an industrial business owner and landlord.

Hobbies over the eons have included stamp collecting, genealogy, Sci-Fi books and magazines, pewter cups, figurines and other miscellaneous items, and growing Roses. In the early 2000's he re-acquired an interest in Photography when one of his numerous children asked him to shoot their wedding photos. No longer having the equipment from his previous marriage, he started fresh in the digital age, with first Fuji, and then progressing to Nikon systems.

Looking for a change after years of capturing beloved family portraits, panoramic landscapes and fascinating architecture, he found enjoyment in photographing women, with an inclination towards Pin-Up style. It was then that he decided to start his photography hobby-company, SydelineWorks Photography.

Having the good fortune of meeting and becoming friends with the twosome of Tia Tormen and her fiancé CK Stone. His photography has blossomed to the point that publishing a book has become a reality. The opportunity of turning his unique photography styles into a paying vocation is within the realm of possibly and the next step for this near-senior citizen.

If you have made it this far through the bio, then you are either Captivated by my intriguing wit or bored. Might I suggest you go peruse the photos of the lovely, entrancing women that are enclosed within the pages of this book instead

Hope you have enjoyed my Photos. With Love............. Amora

Hometown: Pittsburgh, PA
Age: 21 and looking B.E.Autiful
Height: 5'5 with long legs
Measurements: Bust :33B Waist :26 Hip :32
Describe yourself in one word: Exceptional
Who is your favorite Author? I don't necessarily have a fav author, I just like to read in general. Realistic fiction, fantasy and poetry just to name a few
What is your favorite Book? A World of Ideas- Lee A. Jacobus. I read this book in college and fell in love.
If you had only one wish to make, what would it be? Superpowers... lol...and one of the powers has to be the ability to surf thru time. That way I can always relive my most cherished memories.... oh and help mankind ^_^
On Working with Mark: it was definitely a new experience and I was a little shy at first but once they got the music flowing, i just got lost in the colors and at that moment the shyness went away, Then we created magic.
People have always asked, How do you do "it" .Well to get better in front of the camera i do some sexy work behind the camera as well. Alongside my co-founder Kalvin, we've created our baby OVOXO Photography. Which I give thanks to Mark and Tia for not only the help but the inspiration.

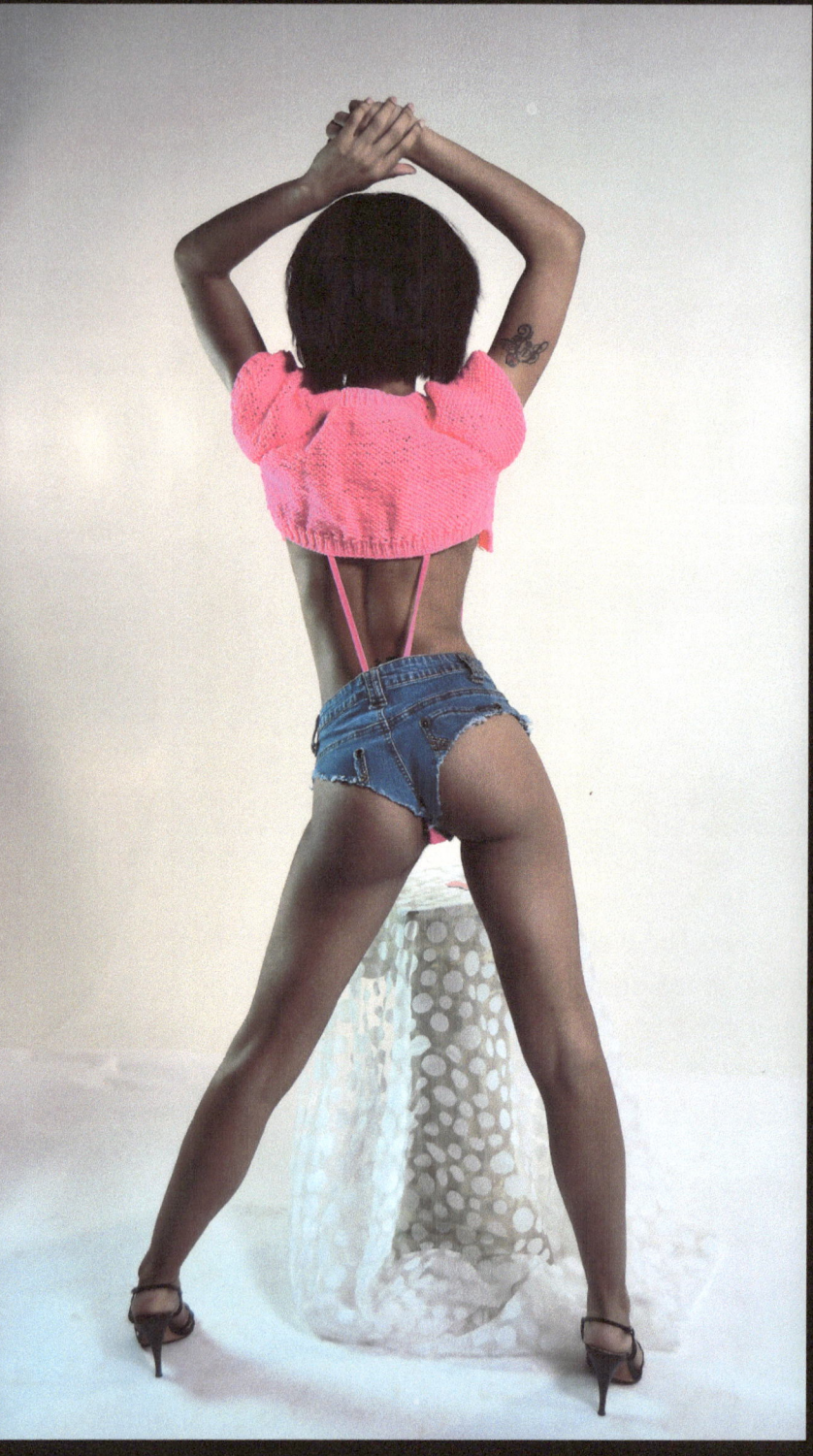